T407
1069
KT-435-809
(Tra)

EM

WITHDRAWN

WITHDRAWN

CATALOGUE

MAROLD BRIDGES LIBRARY
S. MARTIN'S COLLEGE
LANCASTER

WITHDRAWN

By the same author
HELPING THE AGGRESSIVE CHILD: How to Deal
with Difficult Children

HUMAN HORIZONS SERIES

THE BULLYING PROBLEM

*How to Deal with
Difficult Children*

ALAN TRAIN

CARLISLE

HAROLD BRIDGES LIBRARY
S. MARTIN'S COLLEGE
LANCASTER

*A Condor Book
Souvenir Press (E&A Ltd)*

Copyright © 1995 by Alan Train

The right of Alan Train to be identificd as author
of this work has been asserted by him in accordance
with the Copyright, Designs and Patents Act 1988.

First published 1995 by Souvenir Press
(Educational & Academic) Ltd,
43 Great Russell Street, London WC1B 3PA
and simultaneously in Canada

All Rights Reserved. No part of this publication
may be reproduced, stored in a retrieval system,
or transmitted, in any form or by any means, electronic,
mechanical, photocopying, recording or otherwise without
the prior permission of the Copyright owner.

ISBN 0 285 63255 8

Photoset by Rowland Phototypesetting Ltd,
Bury St Edmunds, Suffolk

Printed in Great Britain by
The Guernsey Press Co. Ltd, Guernsey, Channel Islands

*To my wife Vivienne
and with gratitude our parents
George and Winnie Train
Chris and Freda Calvert*

Contents

Part One

DEVELOPING AN APPROACH

1   Being Concerned

AVOIDING THE ISSUE

If you are anxious about your child's difficult behaviour and think that this could be linked to bullying, you have shown initiative and courage in choosing to read this book. Most parents would prefer to deny that the child they love might be a victim; and they would feel ashamed if they knew he was a bully. The thought of a child being a victim is extremely upsetting; to consider that a child might be a bully, and universally disliked, is even harder to contemplate.

However, if you are a typical professional who works with children you will regard bullying as so much a part of a child's life as to be the norm. You know that it is commonplace, and you do not usually pay much attention to it. In taking the trouble to read this book you have therefore shown a genuine commitment to your work.

Experts are concerned that most parents avoid facing the issue of bullying, and that professionals tacitly accept it. Studies clearly show that thousands of children are suffering pain and humiliation daily. Furthermore, the effects are seen later in life: victims may become loners and driven to suicide; bullies often turn into hardened thugs; and both victims and bullies often become involved in crime.

If you are a parent, you are probably reading this book because you have a strong suspicion that your child is being bullied. You may be wondering why he has been late home from school, or puzzled by his sudden reluctance to attend. Maybe you have noticed bruising on his body, and tears in his clothing. He may have become moody and detached. You may be worried and confused about his general unhappiness, and what you should do about it. If you are like most parents you will feel angry and would like to face the bully and give him a little of his own medicine; but you will avoid facing the issue until it becomes serious because, for a variety of reasons, it makes you feel thoroughly uneasy.

If you are a professional, you may have a particular child in your group whose behaviour and performance have suddenly changed for the worse. From being a bright, cheerful child he may have become quiet and morose; his ability to concentrate may have suddenly disappeared. He may act in a negative way towards you. Or, you may have a child in your group whose presence has an unnerving effect on the others. You can feel them breathe a sigh of relief when he leaves.

You may acknowledge these bullying indicators but be unsure about whether or not it is advisable to do anything. You may feel that once you start to interfere there will be no end to it. You would rather allow children to fumble through their relationship problems; you prefer to believe that it is simply part of the developmental process.

Perhaps the unease experienced by both parents and professionals when they encounter bullying springs from an underlying ambivalence towards the issue. Although most people have an innate dislike of bullies, they do admire and envy dominant personalities for the power that they hold. If they had a choice for a child to be either passive or assertive, most would prefer the latter. Perhaps this could be explained as a natural and deep-seated inclination towards survival, or perhaps it has its roots in their personal experience. In any event, it is the perception of most adults that dominant personalities are happier people. They do not appear to be as helpless as others; others need them and come to rely on them. Adults would prefer to have strong children who would be capable not only of looking after themselves but of caring for them, the parents, in later life.

If you have a child who could be a bully or a victim, you may feel responsible for his behaviour. Any notion of him being a bully may be consciously or subconsciously seen as a reflection of your own personality, or of the way in which you have reared him. If you know that either you or your partner has an aggressive, dominant personality, or that your child has witnessed persistent violence, then you may feel accountable. His behaviour may appear to reflect everything that you hate in yourself or in your relationships. For any of these reasons, you may feel that you are to blame for your child's behaviour.

If you can appreciate these issues, it is important for you to resolve them, and in Chapter 4 I shall be discussing how you might do this. It is always necessary for you to look at yourself if you are to be effective with children. For the moment you may like to ponder on whether you can, from your position of maturity, distinguish between a strong personality and a bully. Asking yourself questions like this can help you to crystallise an effective approach to bullying.

If you are a professional you will appreciate the need to have not only a clear perception of bullies and victims, but an understanding of the feelings of their parents. If you have no children of your own, or if you have children who have caused you no great heartache, try to imagine the courage parents need if they are to face up to these matters.

Both parents and professionals need to carefully examine their personal attitude to bullying if they are to help the children involved. Most people treat it in a very casual way. This can be observed in the way they speak to children about their behaviour: very often, without thinking, they encourage them to bully, or condemn them for being passive.

Common excuses
Perhaps it is because of our guilt feelings that we tend either to deny the existence of bullying or to play down its potentially devastating effect on the lives of our children. In our effort to do this we rationalise the matter in a number of ways. As you read the following, ask yourself how many times you have made these comments, and whether you will use them again.

'Boys will be boys.'
This is a comment commonly used to justify instances of boys misbehaving—and, often, when they have been bullying. It seems to be a way of saying that it has nothing to do with them or with you—it is just the way things are. It is a way of passing responsibility on to society as a whole, a neat way of avoiding doing anything about it. And it helps you to cope with the fact that your child might be a victim or a

bully. You take refuge in the mistaken but convenient, and therefore popular, belief that males have certain behavioural characteristics about which nothing can be done.

Such sexist thinking pervades our approach to the serious problem that bullies present, and does nothing to help either them or their victims. We directly encourage boys to be aggressive whenever we make such remarks.

We do much worse with very young children, by expressing satisfaction and pride when we see them dominating others as they play. In doing so we teach them that aggression can be pleasing in itself. Reinforcement by half-hidden adult laughter and a lack of admonition is extremely potent. Young children absorb far more of our values than we care to imagine.

'Girls go through these funny stages.'
It is not only boys who have to suffer the consequences of irrational adult approaches. When girls are bullied they are regarded as over-sensitive and temperamental; and if they bully, they may be said to be in high spirits and full of life. Girls will be girls as much as boys will be boys, and more than this—we perceive them as going through inexplicable 'funny' stages, and how bitchy and catty they are!

This distorted generalised perception of girls prevents us from seeing what is really happening, and we must make a determined effort to view their affairs objectively. Girls as much as boys may begin to believe that it is their fault when they are bullied and nobody seems to notice; if their cries for help are not recognised, they may suffer untold misery.

'It's just part of growing up. It's good for you.'
This is a particularly irrational attempt to console the victim. When you speak like this you are talking as an adult who has long forgotten the pain and fear felt as a young child. You are looking at bullying in retrospect. Have you forgotten the humiliation when you were taunted about your new shoes, or when you were publicly assaulted in your early teens? Try to remember a time in your childhood when you were bullied. Think how you felt. If you find this difficult, it could be because you have chosen to forget.

When you make this comment to a child you are telling

him that bullying is acceptable and that if he is unable to bear it he must be abnormal. In doing so you may be scarring him for life. You will certainly be defining his relationship with you.

What kind of relationship between you and your child will be promoted by this kind of comment?

Do you think that it will make him feel that you care?

'Go and fight your own battles.'
This dismissal is usually accompanied by precise instructions on how to retaliate. Fathers often show their child how to perform some shifty move ending in a rabbit punch or a half-nelson.

If you treat your child in this way, what do you imagine you are really teaching him?

You are teaching him two things: first, you are teaching him that he cannot turn to adults for help without feeling full of shame; second, you are teaching him how to be aggressive. You are telling him that unless he can overcome the bully he will not have your approval. You are also telling him that the only way to do this is for him to use physical force. This is a dangerous tactic, for you may well lose your child. If he overcomes the bully using your advice, he may begin to see himself as an aggressor. If he is unable to take your advice he will feel that you regard him as some kind of wimp. In either case, you are likely to lose his affection.

'Don't tittle-tattle.'
This response to a child who asks for adult assistance is usually rooted in idleness and lack of interest. One subtext is that the adult couldn't care less about her child's problems; another is that there are more important things to be concerned about. The child is again being given the message that bullying is acceptable and that it is something to which adults pay scant attention.

Can you appreciate why his behaviour might begin to deteriorate?

If he is courageous enough to return to the group he may, because of his anxiety, end up fighting. Alternatively, as a result of your inaction he may become fearful of mixing with other children. By your behaviour you will, of course, be discouraging your child from communicating with you, and the way in which he relates to others may be permanently affected.

To avoid all of these possible consequences you would have needed only to listen, not even to have taken sides.

'Look at me—I was bullied, and it never did me any harm.' The most likely reason we use irrational excuses is that this is precisely how our parents reacted to our complaints. This comment, like many others, is passed from generation to generation without any thought of its implications. Never say, 'Yes, and look at me—I'm all right' in respect of anything. A self-righteous attitude makes you unapproachable by adults, never mind by your child.

Have you never noticed that when you do say this to adults they invariably make no comment. (Think about this one!)

'Ignore it and it will go away.'
Parents and professionals often feel that if they ignore bullying it will stop. They may have vague memories of this being a basic principle of 'behaviour modification'. Regrettably, children are not born with this kind of knowledge! But they are the ones who have to suffer until such time as they learn, usually by trial and error, how to cope with bullies. And some of them never recover.

Often connected with this way of thinking is the belief that if you talk to children about bullying you will be introducing them to a topic that might never have crossed their innocent minds. This is indeed muddled thinking: bullying is part of children's lives; it is not an invention of adults. It occurs in nurseries, playgroups, junior schools and senior schools. When it is openly discussed and where there is an effective anti-bullying policy, it rapidly dissipates. When it is ignored, complications arise: children may be physically beaten by the bullies, and, if nothing else, they will be confused by the indistinct and disparate messages transmitted to them.

By considering your use of these and other comments you have begun to reassess your approach to bullying. You may, though, still doubt the wisdom of interfering in your child's affairs. You know that if he is to grow up and stand on his own two feet he does not need too much cosseting. This is an understandable feeling if he appears reasonably happy, and if you have no deep worries about him. If, on the other hand, you are concerned about his behaviour and feel that he may be involved in bullying, then you do need seriously to assess both your approach and his behaviour.

Because of their innate disposition, some children are more likely than others to become involved in bullying, and as the most effective approach to the problem is for each of us to be aware of the full range of possibilities, it is essential to be able to estimate any potential problems. If parents and professionals know that a child is particularly prone to becoming involved in bullying, they will be in a position to safeguard against it. Prevention is better than cure.

The following exercises should help you to assess the possibility of a child being a bully or a victim. Remember that the exercises cannot tell you whether this is in fact the case: they will only indicate whether he is especially vulnerable in this respect.

If you are a professional, read the following as though you are the parent of a child who is giving cause for concern. Do not simply note the characteristics of bullies and victims, but try to imagine how parents feel as they face these issues.

FACING THE ISSUE

Could my child be a bully?

It is not easy to identify a bully. While the most commonly held perception is of a person who is physically large and threatening, he or she can in fact be small, weak and timid. Using non-physical techniques, he or she may bully other children to assert him- or herself.

Another popular view is that a bully is usually a well integrated member of a gang; but while this is often the case, he or she could be a complete loner. It is hard, and dangerous, to generalise.

However, bullies have one common characteristic: they all bully! We can therefore most readily identify them by their behaviour.

Exercise time

Do not rush the following exercises: the idea is for you to dwell on the issues they raise and to come to your own conclusions about your own child. If you want to benefit from them, you will need to spend at least fifteen minutes on each. Your responses will indicate to you whether your child might have a tendency to bully. More importantly, they will help you to decide exactly what it is about his or her behaviour that worries you.

If you feel brave enough, recruit the help of a friend to perform these exercises. This may put your opinions in perspective. You may find that talking about your child to someone who understands is enough to make you strong enough to cope.

EXERCISE ONE
Answer the following questions:

1   Does my child deliberately try to hurt others and cause them distress?
2   Does he appear to gain pleasure from doing so?

Comments

1   It is difficult to assess the intention of a child. When you are attempting to do this be aware that you might be projecting your fears and worries into the situation; be aware, also, that you may be tempted to make excuses for your child. Quote at least six instances that support your case.
2   You will be able to tell whether your child enjoys hurting others by his reaction at the time and his lack of remorse afterwards. He may appear to be very sorry—but ask yourself whether this is genuine concern or whether he is protecting his best interests.

When you are arriving at your assessment *bear in mind that* bullies consciously desire to hurt others and appear to gain pleasure from doing so.

EXERCISE TWO
Read the following checklist and tick those behaviours that apply to your child:

	rarely	some-times	fre-quently
Punches, kicks			
Grabs, pushes			
Fights			
Teases, taunts			
Makes 'personal' remarks			
Spreads malicious rumours			
Makes threatening gestures			
Makes sexual gestures			
Makes racist gestures			
Intimidates by his presence			
Acquires belongings by threat			
Organises racketeering			
Isolates individuals			
Isolates racial groups			
Isolates gender groups			

Comments
All these activities may be regarded as part of a child's normal development unless they are persistent and pervasive. When you are assessing your response to them you will need to ask two more questions:

1   Does the behaviour occur in all situations when you are with him, or does he behave this way only at certain times and in certain locations?
   If you can be specific about times and locations you may have found an immediate solution: try avoiding these particular ones, and in doing so provide opportunities for success, not failure.
2   Does he behave this way with people other than yourself? If he behaves well only with certain people, look carefully

at the way in which these people relate to him. How do those who experience none of his problem behaviour cope with him? What do they do that is different?

In your assessment *bear in mind that* bullies consciously desire to hurt others and appear to gain pleasure from doing so; and that they are likely frequently to display one or more of the above behaviours in a variety of situations and with a variety of people.

EXERCISE THREE
Read the following checklist, and tick those characteristics that you consider to be dominant features of your child's personality:

	no	yes
Excessively aggressive with peers		
Excessively aggressive with adults		
Excessively aggressive with siblings		
Has poor levels of concentration		
Hates school and teachers		
Physically strong		
Very active		
Assertive		
Unpopular		
Has low confidence		
Has few likeable qualities		

Comments
As in Exercise Two, ask yourself whether these characteristics may be seen in a variety of situations and whether they are observed when your child is with other people.

Bear in mind that bullies consciously desire to hurt others and appear to gain pleasure from doing so; that they are likely frequently to display one or more of the behaviours in Exercise Two; and that they could have at least one of the above personality characteristics.

*　　*　　*

You will now have arrived at some conclusions about your child's tendency to bully. You have asked yourself some searching questions, and I hope that you, and your friend, have arrived at some truthful answers. Do remember that all of this behaviour may be displayed by any child: it is only when it is persistent and when it pervades your child's life and your perception of him that it becomes significant.

In any case, to have been able to conclude whether or not your child is a bully is not the main purpose of these exercises. Although many parents and professionals gain reassurance from putting a label on the child, the important part of the process that you have undertaken is the identification of his behaviour. Even at this early stage you may be able to say when and where he appears to behave in a certain way. You may have concluded that he behaves in this way only when he is with you.

You are beginning to arrive at a position where you can offer valuable help. And your involvement will prove, later, to have been of great value. Bullies are affected by their bullying later in life, and often feel worthy only of punishment. They may feel isolated and become depressed. They may lack self-confidence and be full of resentment that they were not helped when they were younger.

You may soon be able to prevent this happening to *your* child—and even more than this: you may prevent him from leading an adult life of violence and crime. Your efforts may even reach into the next generation, for many aggressive children have modelled themselves on aggressive, bullying adults.

Could my child be a victim?
You are probably reading this book because you suspect that your child is being bullied. You feel for him and want to help. If your situation appears serious and you have given up hope, you may have reached the conclusion that he has brought all the misery upon himself. It may interest you to know that this is how many bullies regard their victims! Although there *are* children who provoke others to bully, they form a very small minority.

Do not cloud your thinking in this way. Forget the notion that your child brings it all upon himself and you will find it very much easier to help him: it would be impossible to do so if you were to begin by looking at him negatively.

There are ways in which you can offer him direct help, which we shall be discussing in Part Two.

More exercises
The following exercises are to help you decide whether your child may be presenting the bully with a vulnerable target. They will not tell you whether he is being bullied; their purpose is to help you to estimate his vulnerability. As with earlier exercises, you will benefit enormously if you are brave enough to share the exercises with a friend.

EXERCISE FOUR
Read the following, and tick those personality characteristics that apply to your child:

	yes	no
Cautious		
Sensitive		
Quiet		
Withdrawn		
Has a negative self-image		
Has a negative outlook		
Feels stupid		
Feels unattractive		
Timid		
Irritating		

Comments
As with the other exercises, ask whether your child displays these characteristics in all situations or whether there are specific times when they become evident. Does he behave this way with others, or just with you?

If the behaviour is specific to a situation, try avoiding it. Remember that you are there to provide opportunities for good feelings, and not trials of strength.

If certain people promote different behaviour in your child

ask yourself how they do it, and give him every opportunity to be with them. Do not feel jealous.

Bear in mind that victims are usually insecure and anxious. They may also be cautious, sensitive and quiet. They may have a very low self-esteem.

EXERCISE FIVE
Read the following, and tick those items that may regularly describe your child's behaviour:

	yes	no
Liable to cry		
Solitary		
Unhappy		
Detached		
Volatile		
Unable to concentrate		
Achieves low attainment		
Unable to remember things		
Reluctant to go out		
Moody		

Comments
Again, with a friend, debate whether your child reacts this way to all events and in all situations. Does he behave in this way only with you, or is he like this with everyone?

If you can provide examples of precise situations where this behaviour becomes evident, you will be able to think how you might avoid promoting it.

Bear in mind that victims are usually insecure and anxious, may be cautious, sensitive and quiet, and may have very low self-esteem. They will often react by crying, and will appear as solitary, unhappy, detached and volatile; they will be underperforming in their work and see themselves as failures.

EXERCISE SIX
Read the following, and tick those items that apply to your child:

	yes	no
Excels at something		
Excels at nothing		
Physically attractive		
Physically unattractive		
Physically different		
Has a different accent		
Has a speech/hearing impediment		
Has a physical/mental handicap		
New to group		

Other: e.g., mannerisms, unusual
interests, the only one in class to take
music lessons, to be excluded from
RE . . .

Comments

You will definitely need assistance here from your friend, for you will find it hard to select items without being biased. You may also be unable to appreciate why such character-istics might add to your child's vulnerability: in your eyes they may be the very essence of the child you love. You may even be directly responsible: did you, for example, insist that he take violin lessons at school?

Be prepared to acknowledge that you may be the one with aspirations and principles, but that your child may be suffering because of them. You need to be aware of these matters: he can still take his violin to school and not suffer the taunts of the school bully, but you will need to work out how this can be achieved.

These exercises will have helped you to consider whether your child is likely to be being bullied; they may have con-firmed what you already suspected, or revealed aspects of his behaviour that you had never noticed. In any case, you will be better able to say what it is exactly that concerns you about his behaviour, and to assess whether or not you should be concerned.

When you are making your final assessment, *bear in mind that* victims are usually insecure and anxious, may be cau-tious, sensitive and quiet, and may have very low self-esteem. They will often react by crying, and will appear as solitary, unhappy, detached and volatile; they will be underperforming in their work and see themselves as failures. They may often be selected by bullies because of something that distinguishes them from their peers.

SOME REASONS FOR DIFFICULT BEHAVIOUR

Having completed the exercises above, you may feel that there is a good chance that your child is being bullied or that he is bullying. Your worst fears may seem to have been confirmed. (But you will need to read the remainder of the book to be clear about this.)

You also need to consider some common reasons for a deterioration in children's behaviour. The following factors may cause a child to bully or to be victimised, as well as creating other behavioural difficulties. The solution to your problem might become glaringly obvious.

Physical problems

A child—and especially a younger child—may have medical problems of which you are unaware. He may have fallen and banged his head without anyone noticing. He may be unable to hear or see properly, or he may have toothache. He will begin to misbehave as he falls behind with his work.

Older children may be developing physically and may be ashamed to talk about things that they feel they should understand.

They may be taking drugs.

Undiagnosed medical problems or secret fears about medical matters can cause your child's behaviour to deteriorate considerably.

Always consider arranging a medical examination. Not only will your doctor see to your child's physical needs: your child may find it considerably easier to talk to him about any problems he may have.

Schoolwork

Many pupils find schoolwork too difficult, and once they are left behind their behaviour will inevitably deteriorate. Young children will often only start to become excessively aggressive when they begin school. This may be caused by work that is too hard for them, but often it is because they find it difficult to cope with other children. Being in a large group for the first time is not easy.

In the same way, children attending a new school will find it threatening and may begin to misbehave.

Older children may be seriously concerned about their impending examinations, or be unable to take the pressure caused by the expectations of both teachers and parents.

A quiet talk with your child's class teacher might result in a simple strategy to overcome the difficulty; it would undoubtedly help you both to know each other's concerns. If you take the initiative and calmly describe your child's behaviour you may find that it is mirrored at school—or, alternatively, that he is completely different there. In this way you may glean an immediate indication of his problem.

Teachers

A child's behaviour may deteriorate considerably when he feels that a teacher is picking on him. Invariably children are going to dislike certain teachers, and when a child is experiencing difficulty with his work he will often focus on the shortcomings of the teacher concerned. It is always possible that she is bullying him (Chapter 10). An immediate solution is for you to discuss the matter with her. Your approach should be that your child feels that he is being picked on. You appreciate that he may have completely misinterpreted the situation, and you know that he can be a problem . . . But is she aware of a deterioration in his behaviour, and if so what can she suggest?

Needless to say, you should not go to the school ready to bully the staff: your aim should be not only to gain a better understanding of your child's behaviour, but to find out about the approach being taken by the school.

Misdemeanours or crime
Should your child have committed a crime or misdemeanour, no matter how small, he will be very anxious about his secret being revealed. The anxiety will be reflected in his behaviour. If you suspect that he may have taken money from your purse or that he is involved in petty crime outside your home, provide him with an opportunity to talk about it.

Do not take a direct approach. If, as with most children, there is someone in his life to whom he relates particularly well—such as a favourite uncle or aunt—mention your concerns to this person and allow the two to be together. In this way your child might relieve himself of a heavy burden.

Other children
Your child's behaviour could be the result of unpleasant group dynamics. Occasionally he will fall out with friends and be temporarily excluded from groups. This is a normal part of growing up, but it can cause pain and unhappiness.

His relationships with other children will continually change. You will be aware that if he is to learn how to cope with people it is necessary for him to experience this. If he complains, do not dismiss him: listen and reassure. You must also be aware, of course, that if his behaviour changes dramatically and is showing him to be grossly unhappy, he may need more than your reassuring words. You may need to take more focused action.

Relationship problems can be effectively dealt with in group discussions, where hypothetical scenarios are examined. This technique and others are used by teachers in lessons related to personal and social education. If you know of your child's predicament, you could make a quiet suggestion to his teacher (Chapter 10). This is an effective approach to personal issues surrounding bullying: no names are mentioned, but without prejudice each child can address his own agenda.

Clothes
Your child may suddenly begin to behave differently when
you have bought him a new item of clothing that he has to
wear to school. He may become sullen when you insist that
he wear a waterproof in the pouring rain.

As children grow they become very concerned about their
appearance, and you would be well advised not to worry at
all about their clothing as they reach their teens. When they
are younger, though, or when you are unable to afford what
they want, you must be aware of the serious embarrassment
it may cause them when they go to school wearing clothes
that they consider to be 'not right', unstylish, or just 'different'. They are liable to be bullied; alternatively, if they are
feeling particularly sensitive to the comments of others they
will see offence where none is intended, and may bully. In
either case you will see a change in behaviour as their self-
image deteriorates.

If your child is fussy about which clothes he wears, adopt
the following principle: he is allowed to wear anything so
long as it complies with the requirements of the school.

Clothing can become a battleground for you and your
child. Take yourself out of it and allow a neutral third party
to establish the rules. In doing so you will be recognising
that the battle you have with him is really not about his
clothing. It is your relationship that is being tested. And
when he is not at school you should relax in the knowledge
that by allowing him to wear what he wants you are encouraging his personal development.

Clothing only becomes an issue if you make it one.

Family dynamics
Children are very sensitive to family dynamics, and when
you are considering the reason why your child has suddenly
started to behave differently you must always ask whether
there have been any recent changes or upsets in the family
that may have affected him (Chapter 10).

It is important for you to communicate with him and to
let him know what is happening: do not presume that you
can hide major upsets. If you were to do so, he would feel
left on his own again to sort out problems without your

assistance. If you keep him informed, you will be surprised how much help and support he can provide in times of crisis.

General development
Always ask whether your child's behaviour is appropriate for his age. Although it is very difficult to assess this because each child develops at his own rate, there are broad stages of development through which some experts believe we all progress (we shall be examining some of these in Chapter 3).

For the time being, a simple way is for you to try to look impartially at the behaviour of your child's peers. You will probably know, anyway, if his behaviour is very different from theirs. If you are unsure ask one of his friend's parents how their child behaves in whatever respects seem relevant to you, but be prepared for unsolicited comments on your son!

CONCLUSION

Experts differ in their estimation of how many children bully and how many are victims. While some would claim that 6 per cent of primary school children are involved in bullying, others would adjust the estimate to one child in five. The seriousness of the problem is, however, undisputed, and researchers demand that adults take the necessary action to alleviate the suffering of so many children.

It is not long since child sexual abuse was considered unimportant. For those who had not suffered at the hands of abusers it was of no consequence; for those who had been abused it was something to hide. We are fortunate to have been alerted to the issue and to be in a position to take action. In the same way we must now acknowledge the daily pain and suffering caused by bullying to over a million children in the UK. As with child sexual abuse, it is not a new phenomenon; it is simply that as we have grown older we have tried to forget the humiliations we experienced as children. We do this to the extent of denying relief to our own offspring.

In this chapter you have faced the most difficult issues

that surround bullying. You have begun by looking at yourself and at some of the ways in which you may be denying its importance. It is essential for you to be sure of your personal approach to these issues. If you are to be an effective helper, you need to have worked out some underlying principles for yourself.

You also asked whether your own child could be a bully or a victim. It is not easy to do this, and it may have caused you pain. But having managed it, you should now feel that you have cleared an important hurdle and are ready to take the matter further. Moreover, having considered other factors that may cause a child's behaviour to suddenly deteriorate you may now also better appreciate the complexity of human behaviour generally, and be aware of how difficult it is to estimate whether a child is actually involved in bullying.

Ultimately your expertise in determining this will be based on your experience of life and your personal integrity. If, as parent or teacher, you have been able to face the issues raised in this chapter and have genuinely reassessed your attitude to the problem, then you have taken the first important step towards providing effective help for both victims and bullies: you have begun to look at the matter objectively.

In the rest of Part One we will consolidate your commitment. We will discuss the nature of bullying and why it happens; and we will take a further look at how you see yourself in relation to your child. Finally, as we approach practical matters (Part Two) we will examine some of the needs of children, concentrating on both bullies and victims. Don't be tempted to omit Part One, for it is here that you will lay the foundations of your understanding of bullying; only if you take time to do this will you be able to get to grips with what it is and with how you might deal with it.

2 Thinking Objectively

If you are to take effective action against bullying, you need to think very clearly about your objectives. When children are involved in bullying, adults who acknowledge it become upset and are generally ruled by their hearts. They are ready to wreak vengeance on the bully or to give the victim a good hiding for being such a wimp. These feelings are understandable. They are the natural reaction of those who care, and perhaps of those who have experienced the trauma of bullying when they were children.

To follow your natural inclination when dealing with children is often a good idea, but in this instance it could place you behind bars! There are laws that prevent adults from physically assaulting children, and they are there to deter any such impulse. Whenever you sense that you are losing control and that you are living on your feelings, pause for thought. Anything you do or say in this state may be irrational and could have a devastating effect on the relationship you have with your child. A common reaction illustrates this: when she does something to endanger herself how often have you said, 'If you do that again, I'll kill you!'

In your attempt to develop the skill of looking at bullying more objectively, you can do two things: you can examine the views of experts and you can look very carefully at yourself. By considering the views of researchers who are required to take a scientific approach, as well as looking at your own reactions, you will be able to become more detached from your predicament and feel more in control. When you are dealing with difficult children it is important that you feel in control of yourself before you try to control them.

Bullying behaviour stimulates primitive instincts in all those involved. Although teachers and child care workers may be more inclined than parents to look at children from a theoretical, detached point of view, when it comes to actually dealing with such behaviour as bullying they too often rely on natural impulse.

As you read about the nature of bullying and the various forms it takes, think about the child at the centre of your concern and the implications for the way in which you might deal with her. More importantly, perhaps, carefully consider how you feel about the bully and about the victim. I will be asking you to consider some searching questions in relation to this at the end of the chapter.

THE NATURE OF BULLYING

All children display a certain degree of aggression, but not all children are bullies. Bullies are aggressive, but have certain additional characteristics.

A conscious desire to hurt

We all need to be aggressive to survive, and the younger we are the more direct the aggression that we tend to display. As we grow older we rely on increasingly sophisticated forms of aggression for defence and acquisition.

Bullies are aware when they hurt others. They do not act as young children may in play, when they may be aggressive in order to acquire belongings or to defend themselves. They do not act as older children may and display an achieving, aggressive style as part of their move towards self-identification. Their aggression has an intent, and it is to cause someone harm. It can occur at any age.

Pleasure in hurting others

Bullies appear to enjoy hurting others. Although all children may be aggressive at one time or another, it upsets most of them when they are so. Following an outburst they will show signs of genuine remorse; and the more they are aware of the inappropriateness of their loss of control, the more remorseful they become.

Bullies show few regrets for their actions; they seem to derive satisfaction from causing harm to others. Because of the pleasure they experience, their bullying is self-reinforcing.

Strength versus weakness

When children who are of equal physical and psychological strength quarrel or fight, bullying is not taking place. It is when one of them is much stronger, and conscious of the other's weakness, that he is bullying. In normal play children test each other; in rough and tumble they become aware of their own strengths and the capabilities of their peers; in fantasy they learn to control their emotions; in games with rules they come to appreciate that each has his own capabilities.

Bullying is happening in any form of interaction where it is clear that one of the participants is incapable of defending himself and where it is equally obvious that the other, being fully aware of this, persists in causing distress.

The common image of a bully is of a large boy whose very presence may threaten others, and indeed it is the case that bullies are usually physically stronger than their peers. However, it should not be presumed that most strong boys are bullies: there is no evidence that large boys are any more aggressive than others. What is significant, though, is that physically strong boys are popular and that physically weak boys tend not to be. If a boy is physically strong he is less likely to be bullied because he is able to defend himself; if he is weak, he is more susceptible to being bullied.

Later we shall be looking at bullying among girls (p. 31), where physical factors play a much smaller part.

Persistent behaviour

At some time all children display the behaviour of a bully. Part of the growing process is learning to gauge how much aggression is acceptable, and we gradually learn to modify our behaviour. We all have the capacity to act like a bully, and even as mature adults we occasionally do so: at these times people may accuse us of bullying. If we were to persist with this behaviour for any length of time they would assume that we were gaining enjoyment from it and say that we were a bully. The hardened bully is one who persistently enjoys causing distress to those around him.

He may have other, attractive, qualities: he may be intelligent, and he may respond very well in the presence of a controlling adult. But left to his own devices he will torment those weaker than himself. To those around him he is someone to be feared because of his persistent tendency to cause distress. Even when he is not present, he is a latent threat.

Groups and individuals

Groups can bully, and so can individuals. Many children who would not normally be aggressive will associate with a strong bully and in a group adopt his tactics. They will have fewer inhibitions when they see the bully gaining pleasure from his victories; as part of his gang, they will feel less responsible for their actions. Bullies gain prestige and status from those around them; they often actively recruit and can provide others with an opportunity to bully. They may be regularly accompanied by two or three henchmen who seemingly admire and support them.

While children normally play in groups and sometimes cause distress to members or to non-members, bullying occurs when the group persistently causes harm to either individuals or other groups less resilient than itself. We all like to feel that we belong, and many weaker children are attracted to the bully gang; the intensity of its purpose adds to its appeal.

Group bullying is often performed by organisations that have racial or religious orientations. The zealous pursuit of their aims involves the derision and annihilation of other cultures and beliefs. They recruit children for their purpose, and are capable of killing to achieve their objectives. Poorer inner-city children with a tenuous sense of belonging are attracted to their distinctive policies of intolerance and their direct physical approach.

Anxious bullies

It is often assumed that children who bully are anxious individuals who bully because of their underlying insecurity. Although there are such bullies, most would appear to have normal levels of anxiety; moreover, they do not generally display an exceptionally low self-esteem.

Bullying would appear to be a consistent personality trait: the indications are that at any age bullies are aggressive not only to younger children but to their peers and to adults. Taking these factors into account, we may conclude that by nature some children are more inclined to bully than others. We shall be examining the reasons why children bully in Chapter 3. For the moment, consider the treatment implications of the research findings just outlined. If they dishearten you, do not despair.

If you know that a bully is anxious, you may wish to provide a morale-strengthening programme. If, on the other hand, you accept that a bully is not an anxious child, you may want to offer him specific help in 'the feeling states', and supplement this with training in social skills.

Antisocial behaviour

Bullies are generally involved in other antisocial behaviour while they are still at school. They abuse staff, steal belongings and vandalise property. They promote a negative attitude to school among other children, and are the root cause of much truancy. They may display a bullying approach to adults and children outside school, in this way tarnishing the school's image and eroding the desire of other children to belong to it.

Young bullies and their victims may develop serious psychological problems; later they may experience distress as they come to terms with shame and guilt. In consequence, as they progress through adolescence, they may become more alienated from society. Thus, young bullies and victims who are not helped may develop into adolescent thugs and hardened criminals. Children who bully in junior school are four times more likely than others to be involved in serious crime by the time they are twenty-four; their victims are equally at risk.

FORMS OF BULLYING

Physical bullying

When we think of bullying we tend to see it in its physical form. Our minds are filled with images of large boys inflicting physical pain on weaker pupils. We think in this way because this is the form of bullying that can be life-threatening. As young children, we may have been able to withstand the taunts of the bully as long as they were not accompanied by the very real possibility of physical violence.

Also, physical bullying registers in our minds because it is more visible than other forms: scratches and bruising provide concrete evidence. However, much physical bullying occurs in secret, and when that happens there are no such obvious indicators. Persistent digs in the ribs when pupils are standing in line and constant kicking under the classroom table go unnoticed; the evidence is rarely presented.

Bullies gain pleasure by creating distress in others; because it is self-reinforcing, inflicting minor physical injury can escalate to committing serious assault and even murder.

Verbal bullying

In Chapter 1 we looked at some familiar comments that we resort to in our attempt to avoid the issue of bullying. A popular cry usefully noted here is one regularly directed by children at their bullies: 'Sticks and stones may hurt my bones but calling doesn't hurt me!' By persistently chanting this when verbal bullying is taking place, children are trying to reassure themselves that they will survive. The tag has been supplied to them by parents who, in their maturity, can appreciate its value. Regrettably, young children who are in the process of formulating a sense of identity are not in a similar position. Verbal bullying can be extremely hurtful to them, and can seriously impede their personal development.

As children develop they begin to crystallise a concept of self, and it is essential that during this time they be given a great deal of support and encouragement. They definitely do not need harsh criticism or vicious verbal abuse. In the course of growing up, they become increasingly concerned about their physical appearance and spend much time on personal grooming. They are sensitive to their health and general physical condition. They are concerned about their performance in games and academic work, and are very aware of their own personality traits.

The verbal aggressor hits hard at these soft spots; his comments have an added potency for the victim, since they come from another child rather than an adult.

Racial bullying
When bullies make racial comments they are deriding not only the personal qualities of the victim but everything else that constitutes her personality: her family, her culture, her home and her origins. The bully mocks all of these and attempts to make his victim feel ashamed. Verbal abuse can take the form of racist graffiti in school toilets. Another form of racial bullying can be seen in derogatory written material that is usually disseminated in schools by racist groups who recruit young children to their bully gangs.

Verbal bullying of racial groups and individuals can escalate into physical violence and murder.

Bullying by gestures
It is not necessary for a bully to strike for you to be afraid. In many ways the thought of being assaulted is more frightening.

Bullies often make threatening gestures to others. Fists and grimaces can be particularly effective, and as they are made in silence they carry much less of a risk for the bully. Other gestures may mock the attitude of a willing pupil. For example, two fingers in the mouth, denoting physical sickness, deride anyone who has given an exemplary reply to the teacher's question. Racial and sexual threats made in full view of other children when the teacher has her back turned are especially hurtful and embarrassing for the victims: it is not easy at the time for them to do anything about it without taking enormous risks with peer relationships.

Extortion bullying
The bully will often extort personal belongings from other pupils, and for this purpose will threaten them with physical violence or blackmail. Many children take food or money

to school for their lunch. They invariably have calculators and other pieces of equipment in their schoolbags. Their clothing may be in vogue; their bicycle may be the latest model. The bully chooses what he wants, and places his victim under threat.

It is not only material belongings that he wants: he may require goods of another kind—for instance, a homework assignment done, or sexual favours granted. He acquires these by intimidating the victim with threats of physical violence or malicious rumour.

Exclusion bullying
Bullies often do nothing particularly noteworthy. Rather, what they do *not* do may constitute their tactic. For instance, they do not speak to their victims, or include them in group activities. This is extremely hurtful, since all children attend school not only to study but to gain the benefits of belonging to a social group. The friendship and good opinion of their peers are vital anchor points for successful development. If children are rejected by their peers they can be devastated. No one knows this better than the bully, and she focuses on it to great effect. She will gain ultimate satisfaction by belonging to a group from which her victims are excluded.

Isolating a person is to condemn her to introspection and self-doubt. The bully does this deliberately and gains pleasure by persuading others to join her. She will spread rumours about her victims; she will distinguish herself by her persistent taunts and derogatory remarks about those absent from the group.

BULLYING IN SCHOOLS

Whenever large groups of children gather together there will always be some who act in an excessively aggressive way. Bullying, therefore, occurs in all schools and at all ages. No school should deny the existence of bullying: if it is not seen it will be because it is not being acknowledged. In Part Two we will be taking another look at some of the following issues, and describing more fully the ways in which they may be approached. I cannot resist, though, offering here some

initial suggestions for your consideration: I am sure you will
find that others spring to mind.

Secrecy

Most bullying takes place in secret. The bully is conscious
of the unacceptable nature of her actions, and the victim is
ashamed of her status and fearful of reporting the aggressor.
In many schools there are hidden recesses where victims
may be cornered; in all schools there are, in such places
as toilets and changing areas, private opportunities for
bullying.

Bullies will always find a place and time to practise.
Because of the impossibility of providing constant adult
supervision, the easiest way to combat bullying is by
recruiting everyone in the school for this purpose. When
every child and member of staff is clear about what to do
about bullying, and when none feels shame in taking the
necessary course of action, bullying will have lost its secret
hiding-place.

The children's ages

Bullying may occur in nursery school; though children at
this age are unable to appreciate the concept, their parents
confirm that it takes place. It also occurs in junior and secondary schools. However, as children become older bullying
decreases and changes in nature: it becomes less physical
and more verbal. Younger pupils are thus more exposed
to bullying: they are inexperienced and vulnerable to the
attentions of the bully, who may often be an older and larger
pupil.

So keeping age groups separate is desirable; one-room
schools with a wide age range offer a potential breeding
ground for bullies, as do all-age playgrounds.

Class size

The size of a school or class would appear to have no bearing
on the amount of bullying taking place, but the age composition and the chemistry of the group in terms of academic
attainment, psychological resilience and other factors

determine the dynamics, and are therefore significant. Also, large unsupervised group settings create optimum conditions for bullying in schools (see p. 31, playtime).

Whatever its size, a class should be seen in terms of sub-groups: teachers should be aware that they may be promoting bullying by paying insufficient attention to the grouping strategy that they employ.

Groups should be organised in such a way that the self-esteem of each pupil is promoted. For this purpose pupils should always be placed in their chronological age group, whatever their level of attainment or ability. The need for certain vulnerable children to be in a supportive subgroup should not be underestimated. The key to the success of any subgrouping policy is to be found in an accurate assessment of the emotional support needed by each child.

An anxious child who is prone to being bullied would not benefit by being placed in the same group as a bully, just as a bully would be best placed with children who are more resilient.

Travelling to and from school
It is often thought that children are bullied as they go to or return from school. In reality most bullying occurs on the school premises: in classrooms, in corridors or—most frequently—in the playground. All the same, away from the school premises a bully may challenge a victim to fight in front of his henchmen, and he may directly extort money. He may taunt his victim in public, or lie in wait as the child takes a set route to his home. So the victim is exposed to the attentions of the bully in both corners and wide-open spaces.

Those who travel on school transport are often trapped in a situation from which there is no escape. They must survive in a large group of mixed-age children, with minimum adult supervision: another golden opportunity for the bully. The idea that transport workers with no relevant training have the qualities necessary to control a large group of children should never be accepted; and in any case it should never be assumed that anyone can do this while simultaneously driving the vehicle.

Playtime

Bullying can take place anywhere in school. Much of it is by whispered threat and gesture and occurs in close proximity to staff. If the bully is experienced enough, knuckles can be silently screwed under the ribs, or flesh can be twisted and burned without a murmur from the victim.

But it is in the playground during breaks and lunchtime that most bullying takes place. This is another time when children meet in large mixed-age groups and with a minimum amount of adult supervision. Breaktimes are often short and do little but promote problems, as children have no sooner adapted to a large unstructured group setting than they have to return to class.

The cumulative time spent on breaks is considerable, and should be seen as a significant part of the school curriculum. But playtime is usually regarded by staff as a time when they themselves can relax; they often pay little attention to the problems that it crèates for some children. With so many in the playground it is not possible for every deserving incident to be given attention: victims are told to go and play, and bullies are allowed to hide.

In the thinking schools, professionals realise that both their own lives and the happiness of their pupils can, with forethought and planning, be dramatically enhanced. Children with bullying tendencies are the only ones who relish the thought of being gathered together en masse. Their victims and their teachers look upon these interludes as little more positive than moments to be survived.

Boys and girls

Both boys and girls are bullied at school. But boys tend to bully more than girls, and are involved in more direct physical assaults either as bully or as victim. It is important, though, to note that both boys and girls suffer more from non-physical abuse than from physical forms, and it is the non-physical forms that tend to go unnoticed.

Regrettably, it is often the non-direct techniques of bullying that are expected of girls, and put down to what is generally regarded as their tendency to be temperamental. Many other forms of bullying are considered a normal part of growing up—for instance, the sexual harassment that boys often indulge in (see below). In this way, a great deal of bullying goes unrecognised; the bully is perceived as acting normally and the victim as being at fault.

It cannot be assumed that single-sex schools provide safer environments. Bullies belong to both sexes, and regardless of where they are they use similar strategies. Because it is so lethal, exclusion bullying is a common technique among girls. When a girl is excluded from her peer group she is devastated: she immediately feels that there is something wrong with her. If a boy is excluded from *his* peer group, on the other hand, he can still maintain credibility. Indeed, boys are often assumed to have greater strength if they exist outside their peer group; even total loners are to some extent regarded in this way. However, girls who are isolated from their peers are accorded no such respect.

Often girls are excluded from their peer group for not complying with its consensus of opinion or its standards of personal presentation. They are not expected, as boys are, to demonstrate their individuality: if they do not conform with the group, none of the other girls will speak to them. Thus a girl either sacrifices her integrity or is ostracised. It is not surprising, then, that when girls are bullied in this way the effects are particularly long-lasting. In most cases rifts are never healed and the victim may find it difficult to form meaningful relationships with other women in the future.

It could be said that because of the expectations of society, girls generally suffer more at the hands of bullies than do boys. Since we expect girls to be temperamental, we often fail to acknowledge the reason for any unhappiness, and we tend to perpetuate the notion that it is only boys who may exhibit strength in their individuality.

Sexual harassment
Because of the sexual stereotyping that pervades society, many girls accept this kind of harassment; they feel uncomfortable, but are uncertain about how they should react. Sexual harassment in co-ed schools can take the form of comments that may be construed as complimentary *or* derogatory, or male gestures that may be regarded as flirta-

tious *or* degrading. Boys can physically harass a girl by rubbing up against her or by touching her in an unwanted way; if the girl objects, she takes the risk of embarrassment when the bully says that it was an accident or merely playful fun.

Particularly hurtful to girls are occasions when their sexual reputation is placed in jeopardy: bullies will often extort favours by threatening to spread malicious sexual rumours about the victim.

Sexual harassment takes place not only in co-ed schools but in single-sex schools too. Boys may be harassed because of their femininity and girls may be taunted because of undefined sexual allegiances. Bullies go to the heart of the matter to cause distress, and will focus on sexual identity and appearance whenever the opportunity arises.

CONCLUSION

There are many forms of bullying, and in this chapter we have briefly looked at six of them in isolation; we have also examined certain predominant characteristics of bullies.

In reality the scenario is far more complex than might be suggested. For instance, a child who is threatened by gestures or words may feel that she has been physically assaulted; when a child is punched or kicked it may be for the purpose of extorting money from her or it may be for the intrinsic pleasure of the bully. In Chapter 3 we shall discuss some possible reasons for bullying, and among other aspects we will consider the part that both parents and teachers play in generally promoting aggression.

But now pause, and consider the implications of some of the rather bare statements made in this chapter about the nature of bullying. To help you do this I have prepared some questions:

Punishment and pleasure
1 If the bully gains pleasure by dominating others weaker than himself, how do you propose to administer his punishment without condoning his style?
2 What is the difference between the action of an adult

and that of a bully, who both impose punishment on a person younger or smaller than themselves?
3 How can you be sure that by punishing the bully you are not reinforcing the pleasure he feels when he bullies?

Perception

1 If you accept that bullies consciously desire to hurt others whom they perceive to be weaker than themselves, how can you use this as a basis for *your* approach to them?
2 If some bullies perceive the world around them as a threat, what would be a guiding principle for you to adopt in your behaviour towards them?
3 If some bullies find it difficult to imagine how other people feel, how would you define your objectives when you are dealing with them?

Belonging

1 If you accept that children join the bully gang because they have a need to belong, do you feel ashamed that whatever you are offering cannot compete?
2 If the bully wishes to achieve status and does this by bullying, can you provide an alternative without appearing to reward him in the process?
3 Do you feel that it is in the bully's interests to be dealt with privately rather than confronted publicly in the presence of his peer group?

Pro-social behaviour

1 Can you think of any way in which the characteristics of the bully can be put to good use?
2 Can you give a bully a conscience?
3 If a bully cannot appreciate the needs of others, would it be better to face him with a consequence for his actions rather than to reason with him?

At this stage these questions may be difficult to answer, but the fact that you are attempting to do so means that you are beginning to look at bullying more objectively. If you are unable to come to any definite answers, do not be surprised. Even the experts have not fully resolved many of these questions, and there is good reason to doubt that they will ever be able to fully explain human behaviour. For the stance that you will take to be acceptable, though, and for it to be a viable starting point from which to help both bullies and victims, you will need to examine all the surrounding issues. Asking yourself difficult questions such as these will help you to crystallise your personal approach.

When you have finished Part One, return to these questions and see if things are any clearer to you.

3 Looking for Reasons

Whether you are a parent or a professional, it is important for you to know why a child might be involved in bullying: you may feel that if you can find out the reason for his unacceptable behaviour you will be able to help him. You may also feel that you are responsible for the way in which he is behaving and that you need to know what you have been doing wrong. Parents in particular feel this way and have strong guilt feelings about their child's behaviour; they also have to contend with the view of professionals, who invariably blame them for everything that the child may thing, say or do.

Whether a child behaves as he does because of the way in which he has been brought up or whether he behaves as he does because of his innate personality has always been at the centre of educational and philosophical debate. As with most aspects of the human condition, nobody will ever be able to provide hard and fast rules: each person is unique in his personal chemistry, and exists in unique circumstances.

THE COMPLEXITIES OF INTENT

We shall be discussing the part that aggression plays in a child's development later. For the moment, it is important to make clear the difference between an aggressive child and a bully.

A child can be aggressive in order to defend himself or to acquire possessions. Some experts would say that the difference between this normal aggression and bullying is to be seen in the reason for the aggression. If a child is being aggressive for the pleasure of the act itself and for the sensation he experiences when he makes a child weaker than himself suffer, he is bullying. If he is being aggressive to defend himself or to acquire possessions from someone no weaker than himself, he is not. He may be being excessively aggressive, but he is not bullying.

I am sure you can sense how complicated this can become. Two questions immediately come to mind:

1 How may you determine whether the antagonists are of equal strength?
2 Would any child attack another if he did not feel that he was somehow stronger?

A further question might be?

3 How can you measure the aggressor's intent or the pleasure he receives from bullying?

Man has pondered on these questions since time began, and in Chapter 4 we shall be looking more closely at your reactions to these and other issues.

Instincts

Some experts believe quite firmly that children are born with strong aggressive instincts: they automatically know how to suck, and have the ability to gain attention without being able to speak. They have an inborn desire to acquire things, to compete and to survive. They have a hunting instinct and a fighting instinct. These qualities and physical reflexes are part of a child's personality when he is born. But in some children, various instincts and reflexes are more developed than in others.

Aggression is one of these instincts. A bully could be regarded as a child who has been born with an excessive amount of aggression.

Another view is that human beings are born with a death instinct, an impulse to destroy themselves, to release themselves from the tensions of life. This conflicts with their equally important need to create and preserve life. Aggression may, then, be interpreted as the result of the death instinct being blocked by the instinct for self-preservation. In this respect the bully might be seen as having an unbalanced mind.

It is not only theorists who propose that aggression is a

built-in feature of human beings. Neurophysiologists have advocated psychosurgery as a solution to violent behaviour, and other specialists have concluded that aggressive responses in boys can be accounted for by their testosterone levels. It is believed by some that various parts of the brain control such impulses as aggression or flight, and that aggression can be induced by the electrical stimulation of the brain's circuitry. There is a growing body of opinion that believes in the use of drugs to control the behaviour of aggressive children.

The bully could, according to these specialists, be regarded as a person who is physically handicapped.

Behaviour

Other experts believe, as mentioned earlier, that all actions are determined by life experience. Thus the bully is a bully because of her experience of life. And when she has bullied, people may have paid attention to her, thus reinforcing her aggression.

Aggressive outbursts are seen by some to be the result of frustration. Thus, when a child is prevented from doing something, she has either a physical or a verbal outburst. Frustration can equally result in a retreat into fantasy. This is regarded as inward aggression and often ignored, since it poses few problems for anyone but the child herself. We all have a need to be frustrated in order to achieve, and so we all have a capacity to tolerate frustration. A child may be excessively aggressive because of a low frustration tolerance.

A child who bullies can therefore be viewed as someone who has learned to gain attention in this way; she may be seen as someone who is unable to tolerate frustration, and who will bully should she be thwarted in her objectives.

Compromise

The position that most theorists and practitioners assume is an amalgam of these two approaches: they say that a child's character is a combination of her unique personality and her experience of the world. She is born with certain qualities, and difficulties experienced in life can create characteristics such as stubbornness or tidiness. In-built tendencies to love and to destroy vary at birth from child to child. From the beginning of life, however, the child also interacts with the world around her.

A bully would therefore be regarded as a child who has been born with a dominant aggressive trait, and who during her childhood has had experiences that have reinforced it.

PERSONAL CHARACTERISTICS AND EXTERNAL REINFORCERS

Bullies
Bullies appear to have many characteristics in common, and these may be seen as the reason for their bullying:

1 They tend to react in an excessively aggressive manner; their behaviour is uninhibited.
2 They have a strong desire for power and dominance over others.
3 They are alienated from the world and regard people in a hostile way.
4 They cannot appreciate that it is wrong to bully.
5 They cannot empathise with their victims.
6 They pass responsibility for their actions on to others: they say that their victims deserve to be bullied.

These characteristics may be *reinforced* by external factors:

1 Uninhibited aggressive behaviour may be promoted and reinforced. Parents may encourage a child, at an early age, to be uninhibited by not providing him with boundaries for his behaviour; they may reinforce his aggression by conveniently construing it as an indication of his leadership qualities.
2 Power and dominance in a child may be rewarded by the acquisition of material goods or by a feeling of increased status and prestige. The behaviour of young children can be modified by rewarding them with desirable objects; the behaviour of older children can be modified by peer approval and admiration.
3 Alienation may be increased, since it too can give status and a sense of identity (see developmental processes, p. 42).

4   A sense of right and wrong can usually be promoted by the clarification of boundaries for behaviour. In a child who cannot tell the difference between right and wrong it may be that he received confusing messages about this when he was being brought up.

5   A bully's inability to appreciate the wrongness of his bullying may be linked with his inability to feel what the victim may be experiencing. This inability to appreciate feelings may have been promoted by traumatic experience when he was a child; it may be reinforced as the bully sees his victim suffer because of sensitivity.

6   The tendency to pass responsibility for his bullying to the victim may be seen as an indicator of the bully's incapacity to look at himself; this may have been reinforced by repeated charges of insensitivity, and by the bully being labelled with the above characteristics.

Victims share many characteristics, and these too can be seen as part of the bullying equation. Bullies choose certain people to bully rather than others. Their victims can be described as passive or provocative victims.

Passive victims
The characteristics of passive victims are in many ways the opposite of those displayed by bullies:

1   They have a high level of anxiety and insecurity.
2   They are cautious, sensitive and quiet.
3   They have a low self-esteem.
4   They have few friends.
5   They have a negative attitude towards violence.

These characteristics may be *reinforced* by certain external factors:

1   A high level of anxiety and insecurity may be promoted and reinforced by an unrealistic level of expectation from parents or teachers.
2   Cautiousness may be reinforced by psychological or physical trauma; sensitivity may be reinforced by parental

over-reaction; quietness may be reinforced by the imposition of unwelcome personal exposure.

3   Low self-esteem may be reinforced by rejection by parents and peers.

4   Friends become fewer as introspection and self-doubt grow.

5   A negative attitude to aggression of any kind is reinforced by the pain of being picked on by the bully and by an inability, because of anxiety, to be pro-active.

All of the above characteristics of the passive victim may be the result of over-protection by the parents, who may have been over-protective because of their personal need for security or because of the obvious fragility of their child. Their over-protection may have reinforced his condition and caused him to be bullied; this, in turn, makes his condition worse.

Provocative victims

There are some children who provoke bullying. Although these are in the minority, their characteristics should be noted. In many ways they appear to combine the qualities of bully and victim. In addition to the characteristics of the passive victim, provocative ones have the following in common:

1   When attacked by the bully they try to retaliate.

2   They may try to attack other children weaker than themselves.

3   They could be described as hyperactive: they are restless and unable to concentrate.

4   They may be clumsy and immature.

5   They may be disliked by others, including teachers, because they irritate and create tension.

The personal characteristics of a child may therefore be seen as both the reason for and the result of his being involved in bullying. They may be induced or reinforced by his personal circumstances and by the reactions of those around him to his condition.

Oddities
Although it is often assumed that bullies victimise children
who are odd or different, this is not proven. Children are
not picked upon by bullies because of the colour of their
hair or because they wear glasses any more than children in
general engage in this kind of behaviour. The reason we tend
to *think* that children are bullied because of their oddities is
twofold: first, among any group of children there will be
a high percentage who are regarded as having oddities;
second, the tendency is to overlook the fact that there are
countless numbers of children who are odd because they are
overweight or because they speak differently, but who are
never bullied.

Bullies may use the oddity of a child to enhance the effectiveness of their bullying, but oddities should not be considered as a reason for their behaviour. The only significant
external factor in bullying is the size and strength of those
involved: bullies pick on those who are physically weaker
than themselves.

DEVELOPMENTAL PROCESSES

Aggression in childhood
From the moment he is born a child relies on aggression.
He needs it to survive. At birth he has bodily needs, physical
feelings and thoughts. He does not relate to people in an
affective way, but sees them as part of his survival system.
He is aggressive and demands unconditional acceptance and
attention to his needs. This is normal, and to be expected.

However, complications at birth may result in some level
of organic dysfunction, and physical illness in early childhood can promote excessive aggression. A child of any age
should be medically examined if he is causing problems; in
infancy an examination is essential whenever he is distressed. Aggression may be associated with physical and
mental disabilities, and should then be viewed as a symptom
of frustration.

When a child is nearing the end of his first year and beginning to interact with others, we see a change in the nature
of his aggression: he begins to use it to acquire toys and

other possessions from his playmates. He starts to impose himself on his surroundings. His centre of attention becomes objects in his environment rather than himself. They are seen as part of himself, and anyone who attempts to take them away is seen as a threat to his person.

As he approaches his fifth or sixth year his aggression changes in quality. He becomes less likely to use physical violence to achieve his aims, and he will react with anger only if he thinks that he is being attacked intentionally. This ability to perceive a person's intent is developed at an early age. Well before he can speak he will be able to receive language: he will know what you mean and what you intend. The child thus develops from an infant who acts aggressively in order to acquire what he wants into a person who acts aggressively only when he feels threatened.

The bully may be seen as a child who has not developed beyond the stage of the infant: his aggression may be seen as providing him with the immediate gratification of his needs. He may be viewed as someone who still has an excessive need to impose himself on his surroundings, or as a person frustrated in his desire to possess objects and people. He may be seen as someone who feels unduly threatened by the world around him.

The victim may be seen as someone who has never achieved his basic needs through aggression. He may have been pacified rather than satisfied during infancy. He may have had objects forcibly and insensitively removed from him; he may, because of confused parental messages, be unable to interpret intent, and therefore unable through fear of failure to commit himself to a direct course of action. He may feel unduly threatened by people, and prefer to withdraw.

Tantrums

Temper tantrums are a normal part of growing up. Children use them in order to achieve their aims. In early childhood the mother responds to the tantrum, but as the child grows she pays less attention to it; accordingly, he begins to use alternative ways of communicating.

Children must learn acceptable ways of negotiating and

communicating, and the tantrum plays an important part in this process. However, if tantrums are left unchecked they can develop into training sessions for bullies. If parents are present, they know when it is time to intervene; they can recognise distress, and should never hesitate to respond.

The bully may be seen as a child who has been unable to develop acceptable ways of communicating and negotiating, and who still gets what he wants by threatening discomfort to others. The victim may be seen as a child who has had too heavy a parental response to his tantrum; he has been over-controlled and reaps rejection rather than reward by being aggressive.

Adolescent aggression

As a child grows, she gradually moves towards independence. From being a small child bonded with her mother she becomes a separate person, no longer reliant on those who brought her into the world. As she moves from childhood to adulthood she retains significant anchor points from her experience of family life. These enable her to benefit from the strengthening process of adolescent stress.

The quest for a sense of personal identity is seen as a central characteristic of any human being. We need to have a firm sense of who we are and what we stand for before we can interpret the world around us: we view everything in relation to ourselves. Our quest continues throughout life, but is seen by some to reach its crisis point in the teenage years.

At this time boundaries and controls are disappearing, as parents play a smaller part in the child's life and as she attempts to make her mark in society. Uncertainty predominates as she floats between having a strong sense of belonging to the children's world and knowing that she is not yet a full member of the adult group. She is in no-man's land, and very vulnerable. As she experiments with personal decisions she begins to sense personal control: she is becoming less helpless and more able to determine her future.

Depending on her personal characteristics and on her life experience, she may take one of two routes: she may retain certain values from her past, or she may reject everything and attempt to make a complete break. If she takes the former route she will achieve a positive resolution: she will feel at home in her own body, she will sense where she is going, and she will feel strong ties with significant people in her life. If she takes the latter, she will achieve a negative identity. She will not be at ease with herself, she will not know where she is going in life, and she will have no stabilising anchor points from the past.

Making a break of some sort is, however, essential. If no break were made, she would remain locked in childhood. The process is necessarily painful, and affects not only the child but those around her—they too must suffer her changing moods and indecision, her heightened sense of injustice and her introspection.

Adolescents are faced with four challenges: they must relinquish some of the values and beliefs they held as a child; they must relive traumas experienced in childhood so that they can master them and not be subject to them for the rest of their lives; they must accept their personal history (since one cannot have a future without a past); and they must create a firm sense of their sexuality. When these four challenges are met there can be growth towards full autonomy and stability. This is gradual, and carries on through adulthood. Parents and teachers can help them by creating opportunities to place the past into perspective. A parent may talk to the child when an opportunity arises; teachers can encourage a child to express her private thoughts in drama, art or writing.

As adolescents progress towards maturity their behaviour may become more inconsistent. Intense beliefs and values may suddenly fade; new values may replace previously declared convictions; and these, in turn, will be refined and adjusted as the young adult begins to fit them into her scheme of things. There may be regression into childhood mannerisms as the ground is cleared for the new values to take root. Questions about personal history may need to be addressed directly and honestly. The young adult will experiment with sexual relationships in order to clarify her sexual status and identity.

The bully, or the victim, may therefore be seen as someone who has been unable to escape from childhood; she may still identify with a significant adult and have been unable to begin the process towards her own sense of self. The anchor points in her early life may have been too dominant. The aggressive child may have identified with an extremely dominant personality; the victim may have been over-protected by an anxious adult.

In another way, the bully may be seen as someone who has left her past behind her: she bullies in a meaningless vacuum; and the victim may be seen as a helpless young adult, weak with indecision as she is caught between child-hood and adulthood. Both bullies and victims may generally be viewed as young people who have had great difficulty in establishing a pro-social sense of identity.

Alienation

All adolescents appear to be alienated from society as they strive to assert their identity. They can become extremely sensitive when they encounter hypocrisy, insincerity, incon-sideration and dishonesty. They will often treat others as they themselves feel they have been treated, and will be intolerant of all around them. Some adolescents react by withdrawing into their private worlds, becoming lonely and unable to achieve any degree of intimacy with those around them. They are extremely distrustful, egocentric and full of pessimism.

The bully of any age may be seen as a person who is alienated from society: he demonstrates this by his capacity to hurt others. The victim may be seen as a person who is equally alienated from society: he shows his contempt by a resignation to his fate.

THE FAMILY

It is the family that can provide children with the sense of security and belonging so necessary for their development as separate and unique personalities. However, it provides not only a protective and nurturing environment, but also a setting in which its members may unleash their emotions. Within the confines of the family, they can react freely and without social inhibition. It is only outside that they must behave in a consistent and controlled way, if they are to remain socially accepted. So it is in the family that a child is most likely to be exposed to aggression and violence, as well as to love and happiness. It could be said that the family provides the safest environment for learning how to cope with human emotion.

Family violence

The extreme and persistent emotions of others can have a devastating effect on developing children. Violent parents may not only create distressing psychological conditions, they may cause their children physical harm. Child abuse by parents and siblings is a common feature of family life in all social classes, and all members of the family may play a part in aggressive interactions. The child himself may be partly to blame. Restless and difficult children can irritate and induce aggression in those around them. Parents can be driven to distraction by a persistently aggressive and annoying child.

Much child abuse is inflicted by men and women in their early twenties, at a time when they have just begun to live independently away from their own families. They may be having difficulty in forming new relationships, and may not be in a position to meet the heavy demands that parenthood places upon them. In their frustration they may become aggressive, inflict violence on others, or withdraw from the world around them. A child will often become the target for their aggression, especially when it is a sickly child and continually crying. He or she may be physically assaulted, emotionally rejected, or both.

Abusing parents may be habitually aggressive and prone to outbursts, or emotionally cold and depressed. Their aggression in one form or another is released against the source of their irritation. Their abuse of their children alienates them from society, and they become isolated and even more aggressive. They may feel helpless, incompetent and at the mercy of their emotions. They are abusers who feel abused.

When a child is abused there is a fair chance that he will himself become an abuser later in life. So it is important to understand the plight of abusing parents and to help them. Only by doing this will the circle of violence be broken. Studies have clearly shown that if parents are helped, the aggressive behaviour of their children diminishes considerably.

Bullies may therefore be seen as people who have been abused. They may have suffered physically and psychologically, and may have adopted the abuser's pattern of behaviour. The abuser may be the most significant role model in their life. Victims may be seen as children who have been abused and who continue to be passive in order to please; they may do so because they have resigned themselves to this role in life.

Mental illness
Should parents have a personality disorder, the whole family may be affected.

Mental disorders can be contagious: over a period of time, one parent may infect the other with a distorted perception of the world. The couple may become socially isolated, and their children will suffer because of their detachment from society and their inability to perceive the world in anything other than negative, threatening terms.

Parental mental disorder can lead to gross marital disharmony. Parents may conflict over child-rearing practices, and they may cease to relate to each other. The pattern of dominance in the family may show little consistency, causing confusion in the child. Mental illness may involve the hospitalisation of a parent, or the removal of the child from the family home. In either case, the separation may be interpreted by the child as rejection. Parents may be irritable because of persistent illness, and their child may accordingly have a negative outlook on life. Parental illness in itself does not necessarily threaten the welfare of a child; the biggest threat is the gross family discord which may be engendered by the illness.

Both bullies and victims may be seen as victims of their parents' view on the world and of their resultant frustration.

Family size
Children who come from large families tend to bully and fight more than children who come from small ones. This may be related to the fact that physical, material and psychological needs are better met in small families. However, there is little evidence to support the notion that the economic status of a family is directly related to the behaviour of a bully. Directly related is parental discord, especially when the child is recruited as an ally by one of the antagonists.

An only child may be over-indulged. She may be regarded as very precious. Her mother may have excessive contact with her and exclude her from all other relationships. She may mother her for too long, prolonging the process of infantile care and preventing her moving towards independence. She may be emotionally dependent on her child, giving her the love of which she herself was deprived when young, or compensating herself for the lack of a relationship with her partner.

In a large family the mother may be exactly the opposite: emotionally drained and physically exhausted, she may have little contact with her children and appear not to care.

A bully may therefore be seen as a child who has experienced gross family discord, and a victim as one who has been over-protected. Both bullies and victims may be seen as having had an inappropriate level of involvement with their parents.

Child-rearing styles
A mother who shows a lack of interest in her son and who has a cold, detached relationship with him will promote his aggression. A mother who is permissive and too tolerant of her son's aggressive behaviour also encourages it. In either case, the mother is setting no boundaries for her son's behaviour, and this is undoubtedly interpreted by him as an indication of her lack of care.

Both mothers and fathers who control their children by physical punishment or by violent emotional outbursts are promoting aggressive behaviour in them. Families who rear well adjusted children supply the right amount of love and involvement; they offer well defined limits for behaviour, and they do not use physical punishment.

Bullies and victims could therefore be said to be the products of families who provide an inappropriate measure of these features of family life.

CONCLUSION

In looking for the reasons why some children bully and why others are victims we considered three factors. We began by looking at the way in which the personal characteristics of children can determine their tendency to bully or their tendency to be victimised.

Bullies are characterised by an inability to tolerate frustration, and a tendency to display excessive aggression. Victims are characterised by a similar low frustration tolerance, but *they* react by withdrawing from the world and being passive. These characteristics can be reinforced by life circumstances and by the reaction of those around them to their behaviour.

Going on to examine the way in which developmental factors may explain aggressive behaviour, we suggested that a bully may be seen as behaving like an infant, seeking immediate gratification for his needs and feeling unduly threatened by everything around him. Victims may be viewed as those who in their infancy never achieved anything through aggression and who were pacified more than satisfied. Both bullies and victims may be seen as children who have not learned to communicate and negotiate in an appropriate manner. Bullies intimidate, and victims feel sorry for themselves. In adolescence both bullies and victims appear as helpless individuals floundering in between childhood and adulthood.

Finally, we examined the way in which the family can produce a bully or a victim, concluding that both may be children who have been abused in their childhood: one models himself on the aggressor, the other remains resigned and passive to the world around him. Bullies and victims may also be victims of the distorted perception of the world held by their parents and of their consequent frustration. They may be victims of family discord and may have been pawns in their parents' lives. Or their behaviour may be the result of inappropriate child-rearing practices.

In the next chapter we shall be looking at the needs of children and thinking again particularly about bullies and victims. Before we begin, you may like to ask yourself three questions that arise from this chapter:

1 Could you ever regard the bully and the victim as handi-capped children?
2 Do you think the bully and the victim are responsible for their actions?
3 Do you think that children may be born evil?

It would be useful to assess whether your answers to these three questions come from your head or from your heart.

4 You and Your Child

PROFESSIONAL SUPPORT

Many parents who are having difficulty with their child simply need to know that there is someone who understands and cares. If they are isolated in a tenement block and have no one to turn to, their difficult child can become too much to bear and they inevitably lose any control they may have had over him. His aggression or passivity increases to the point where the parent reaches the end of her tether: she simply wants him to leave. The more he is out of sight the better.

The most effective way of altering the behaviour of schoolchildren is for the school to work with and support the parents: inviting them to school for a coffee, on no pretext other than that it would be nice to meet them, can be the beginning of a very worthwhile partnership. Some parents will accept and benefit from precise advice on how to rear their children; many need only to strengthen themselves to the point where they can say no to them. If they are to do this, though, they need somebody's help.

We shall discuss how professionals may work with parents in Part Two, but for the moment it would help if both professionals and parents were to consider aspects of life that we all share. Parents share them with professionals; both share them with the bully or the victim.

SOMETHING IN COMMON

Fragility and resilience
We all accept that human beings are born with varying degrees of intelligence; we also accept that we each have our own physical make-up. Some of us are very intelligent, others are not; most are average. In the same way, some

people are physically strong and some are weak, and most of us are somewhere in between. Less common is the notion that we each have an emotional quotient: some of us are resilient, some vulnerable, and most of us balanced between the two.

This emotional quotient is perhaps the most important of all, since it determines our mental and physical performance: top-class athletes are often separated by split seconds— which they explain in terms of how they were feeling at the time. Lesser mortals are emotionally drained, or charged up, as they go about their daily toil. Emotions form the basis for all our lives.

When we receive good news we are elated; when we hear of a tragedy or personal loss we can become so emotionally distressed that we can hardly move. We tend to assess our day in terms of our emotional state. If we have had a good day it means that we feel good about it, and usually it means that we feel good about ourselves.

In any family there may be a child who has a similar level of intelligence to his siblings, and who is just as strong physically, but when it comes to his actual performance at school or elsewhere, he fails. After acknowledging that his intellect and physical make-up create a unique chemistry, and that subtle changes in his life circumstances may have affected him, it becomes clear that he is operating from a different emotional base. His brothers and sisters may be able to cope with life, but he finds it very difficult. He could be said to be a fragile child who is emotionally vulnerable.

You would be surprised if I were to interpret the actions of your highly aggressive, bullying child as being those of a fragile personality, and I am going to refrain from doing so (even though it is my inclination to believe that, although he presents as a supremely self-confident individual, the bully is so fragile that he denies any feelings). I have already stated that research indicates that he does not appear to have the low self-esteem that many people would expect, and that would be an accepted characteristic of a fragile personality. There are anxious bullies who may react in this way, but they are in the minority.

Victims, however, clearly do display low levels of self-esteem, as do certain highly aggressive children, and the theory of fragility works well when we are trying to understand them. The notion is also useful when you are trying to understand yourself. The kind of relationship you have with people, including those closest to you, is affected by the degree of fragility with which you were born. Perhaps of most significance is the fact that emotionally fragile people find it difficult to relate to others: they find the relationships with those who mean the most to them very stressful.

Mother-and-son relationships are therefore often difficult when one or the other has a fragile personality; when both have vulnerable personalities the relationship is tenuous, to say the least. Ask yourself whether this applies to you and the relationship you have with your child. If he is emotionally vulnerable he may appear distant and withdrawn when really he wants to be close to you. He may be passive because he needs the safety of his own private world.

When such a child is confronted with the raw emotions that may be revealed in the family setting he may react violently and aggressively, or become withdrawn. When he is placed in the spotlight he may react in a similar fashion: the last thing he wants is to be under the microscope. The problem is that when you feel that you are getting close to such a child he may turn off, unwilling to bear a relationship which experience tells him will fail, or which, because of his anxiety, he feels might fail.

The aggressive, domineering bully may seem to be just as distant. Perhaps he too has difficulty in getting close to people because of fragility. But if you accept the findings that bullies are not anxious, fragile personalities, you may interpret his behaviour as egocentric: he does not consider the feelings of others because he is solely concerned with himself, the argument goes.

Think carefully about whether you would consider yourself to be emotionally vulnerable. Do you find it difficult to get close to people? Do you prefer to keep them at a distance—especially, for instance, your partner or your child? All of us have these traits to a certain extent. The vulnerable person is at the extreme end of the scale, far from the position of resilience which the bully would appear to assume.

Self-esteem

Coping with failure

Emotional fragility and self-esteem are intrinsically linked. Those children and adults who have low self-esteem are unable to cope with failure. Very often a child who has low self-esteem rips a page out of her notebook if she makes a single error. When she begins to make mistakes and yet leaves the page intact, it can be interpreted as a sign that she is gaining in self-confidence. When a child begins school she may find the work too difficult, or she may find that she is unable to form relationships with other children. As a result, she behaves badly.

Vulnerable children are most likely to have these difficulties and to experience early failure. Their inability to cope with this results in aggressiveness or withdrawal. They fall further behind with their work and assume a negative self-image.

The importance of pre-school education cannot be over-emphasised; vulnerable children, in particular, need to learn how to communicate and negotiate with others (p. 71), and they need to start at the point where they can experience success. Facilities for play and early education can reduce the number of thugs and criminals, who may have developed from bullies or from victims, or cynical subversives (who may have had similar origins). With sufficient early help, every child can be nurtured to maturity. Society does not *have* to produce alienation in later life.

Coping with change

We must all live within a framework of personal rules and schedules; none of us could exist in a vacuum—we would become insane. At the same time, we need to be able to use this basic framework as a platform for movement. Children and adults with low self-esteem have more difficulty than most when it comes to coping with change. Children become upset when the plans for the day are suddenly altered; adults refuse to depart from seemingly meaningless and insignificant routines.

Reassurance
Children who think little of themselves need constant reassurance that they are acceptable. They will bring their exercise book to the teacher every few minutes. Adults who have low self-esteem have a constant need to be 'stroked' with words of comfort, and their conversation is pointed to this end.

When you think of the victim, clearly, you may say that her self-esteem is low. The bully, however, could be said to think far too much of herself and to show too little caution when it comes to making her mark on the world. When you look at yourself, ask whether you feel that your level of self-esteem is too high or too low. How do you compare to your child in this respect? Do you need constant reassurance?

Your ideal model
We all have in our minds an ideal model of what we would like to be; we have a fixed notion of how things should be done and of what things should look like. When we are unable to achieve our ideal model, we can become frustrated and unhappy. What happens with vulnerable people is that they tend to associate so closely with their unhappiness that they may become angry or depressed. They think less of themselves for not being able to achieve their objective. But the problem is never resolved: if they *were* to achieve their ideal model, another would somehow pop up to keep them going.

We all need to accept our ideal models, for they are our inspiration and reason for living. At the same time we need to recognise them for what they are, and not to become frustrated when they are seemingly unattainable. Perhaps the greatest problem in this respect is that not many of us sit down and ask ourselves what our ideal world would be. We become frustrated and angry, disappointed and distressed, because we have failed in relation to a world that we do not really know.

If you wish to resolve personal difficulties, you could start in no better way than asking yourself what your ideal model is. When you have carefully considered what it is, you might then try and establish where it came from. Are you trying to live with the values of your father or your mother, or are you trying to live in the world of a super-hero such as Linford Christie or Madonna? When you have decided, consider how realistic it is, and make the necessary adjustments. You really should be in your own world rather than someone else's.

The bully and the victim can likewise benefit from this approach.

The process is not easy, though. We need a strong self-image but must somehow achieve a realistic view. For example, the image we have of our body is at the centre of how we think of ourselves, and it is important for us to accept it. We may find this difficult because in society attractiveness is clearly projected in a certain way. Moreover, those who are regarded as good-looking are popular and self-confident. Less attractive people are not so popular, and so tend to have their negative self-image reinforced.

Unattractive children and fat children, in particular, are disliked by others. Their self-esteem is therefore low, and this is reflected in their behaviour. If children are insecure about their body image they may retreat into sickness for protection. They may be tired all the time, rather than sick. This usually indicates that they have given up the contest with regard to their ideal physical self-image.

But as children grow, their self-image changes. When they are young their physical appearance, their playmates and their possessions make up the picture they have of themselves. In their later teens value judgements assume more importance. Their personal strengths and weaknesses and any specific behavioural consistencies begin to form their self-image. They think of themselves in terms of hobbies and interests, beliefs and attitudes. Central to their self-image is their relationship with the opposite sex.

When you are thinking of the child at the centre of your concern it would be useful if you could try to see him as he sees himself. You would then be starting at the same point. It would also be useful, of course, to ask yourself how you may be seen by others, and in particular how you may be seen by your child.

Defence mechanisms

When we are threatened in any way we react defensively.
If we are physically attacked we will either fight back or run
away. If our self-image is threatened we use other, non-
physical, methods to defend ourselves. For if we were to
lose this reaction our life would cease.

When we have a strong image of ourselves and of the part
we play in a clearly defined world, we can resist attack. If
we are unsure of ourselves, if our self-image is weak, then
we will interpret many interactions as threat and react
aggressively. We use three main techniques for this purpose:

1   We counter-attack with sarcasm or other verbal ag-
    gression.
2   We distort information to suit our purpose.
3   We avoid what we do not want to hear.

Those who are vulnerable and feel unduly threatened use
these techniques so much that they may adopt them as a
way of relating to others. Negativity and aggression become
their style of interaction. They acquire a reputation for being
antisocial, and assume this as their self-image.

It is important for us all to have a self-image that is clear
and consistent, and we use other techniques as well to
achieve it:

—If we do anything wrong we blame it on external factors
beyond our control. When good things happen, we try to
take credit for them. We can never do any wrong.
—We always exaggerate the part we have played in shaping
events in which we have participated. We hype our own
performance.
—We always assume that someone else is going to have to
change, that the other person is wrong.
—We invent personal handicaps in order to avoid failure.
In other words, the excuses come before the event as a
guarantee of safety.

Vulnerable people use these techniques more than most,
since they feel more threatened. They have a greater need
to maintain consistency.

Another defence mechanism is to use fantasy. We all

create our fantasy world—our ideal model (see p. 56)—in order to help us cope with the world in which we physically exist. The passive personality may stay in his fantasy world; the bully may assume the characteristics of a fantasy model who embodies his aggression (television and films, p. 66).

When you think of the relationship you have with your child, how defensively do you think you both react? Most parents of difficult children regard themselves as being involved in a constant battle. They are always defending themselves. Most of their children see themselves as being under attack.

Invariably, neither parent nor child has defined what it is that they are defending. But they are, of course, defending their self-image: and if they knew what this was and if they were aware of how the other perceived them their difficulties might be resolved.

Material things

Many professionals assume that a lack of material possessions in the home correlates with problem behaviour among children, while some experts would question this. The socioeconomic status of a family has not consistently been found to be the cause of aggression among its children. Both bullies and victims would appear to come from all social classes and conditions. Neither could it be said that more parents from poorer homes rear their child inappropriately. Good parents remain in the same proportion to poor parents as in every other class of society. Although it may not be possible to apply these findings to every part of the world, they do support the age-old notion that material possessions do not guarantee happiness.

Parents should not, therefore, feel guilty when they are unable to provide everything that their child wants; and if they do provide him with everything, they should ask whether this is in his interests or their own. The bully seeks immediate gratification and will be even more of a bully if he always gets what he wants, just as the victim will remain a victim if everything is handed to him on a plate.

Many parents are exhausted to the point where they will do anything to satisfy the demands of the bully or to stop the whines of the victim. But in doing so they are encouraging the very behaviour that they wish to extinguish. If they cannot cope, they should not struggle on; for their own sake and in the interests of their child, they should seek help. Regrettably, though, too many parents feel ashamed to do so, and those who could give them help discourage them by blaming them for their child's behaviour (Chapter 5).

The generation gap

It is important to realise that we are all at different stages of development. Many parents are unable to understand the behaviour of their child simply because they expect her to behave as they do. Most parents have battles with their child as she progresses through adolescence (Chapter 3), and they need to be aware of the processes she is undergoing. They must take into account her particular sensitivity to moral and ethical issues, and be prepared for her reaction to any form of criticism.

Parents sometimes identify too much with their child. They cannot see her as a separate person; they are unable to do anything but live their own life through her. They live under her skin too much, and any chance of a relationship is thus doomed to failure. A relationship takes two people, not one. Furthermore, many relate to their child as another child would: they treat her as a pal when she needs a parent. Regrettably, they confuse her needs with their own. Children do not need adults as children—they need them as adults.

Understanding your child does not mean that you accept everything that he does. In this respect it is even more important for you to see yourself as a person separate from him, as an adult who has the wisdom and maturity to make important decisions. (We shall be talking about how you need to control your child in Chapter 5.)

The most important thing you have in common with him is your need for each other. You need him as a child; he needs you as an adult.

LOOKING AT YOUR ATTITUDE

We began in Chapter 1 by emphasising the need to examine the level of concern that we have for bullies and victims. In the chapters that followed we looked at their characteristics, and at some of the reasons why children may be aggressive. By spending time on the following questions you will be able to assess how far your attitude to bullies and victims may have changed, and perhaps also to assess the part that you play in promoting your child's behaviour.

Your attitude to your bully
1   Do you see your child as loud and obnoxious?
If you see him in this way, he must make you feel weak. If you respond to him by trying to be louder, you will be on a losing wicket. As a younger person, he probably has more strength and determination than you. If you take a rest and decide not to play the game, you may find that his loudness subsides. If you talk to him quietly he may hear you; when you shout he will only sense your anger. As an adult, you should act in an adult way. Look upon him as an immature child, and do not act as a child yourself.

Do not become embroiled in his interactional style; separate yourself from him, and see his loudness as a sign of his troubled state. Do not see his behaviour as a reflection on your own personality—if you do, you will feel under threat and be inclined to retaliate.

When you see your child being loud and obnoxious, ask yourself whether he is really harming anyone or whether he is merely offending you. If you cannot cope with his loudness and domineering, explain this to him, quietly and in private, and he may surprise you with his compliance. If it is possible to give him times when he *can* be loud, you may avoid feeling that he is obnoxious by making yourself absent! It is important to work out a strategy and not to put up with a situation that you find unbearable.

2   Do you see your child as hard and insensitive?
If you see him in this way, first ask yourself how much warmth you need from him. Perhaps you need more warmt

than he can provide. Many parents feel that they do not connect with their child to the extent they would like. Perhaps they are always afraid of losing him, or perhaps they all tend to identify too heavily with their children.

If you feel this way you should relax in the knowledge that, if he could, he would be much closer to you; if he were able, he would appear to be softer and more caring. Bear in mind that he may be more sensitive than you can imagine, and that because of his sensitivity he may be unable to cope with those who mean most to him. Often, in a perverse way, the more your child feels for you the less he is able to express it.

If he says insensitive things to you and acts as a tough guy, try not to respond in a similar way. You are there to provide him with a model of how he *should* behave. All the same, it is important that you do not accept his insults, for you are there as a parent, to provide boundaries for his behaviour. We shall discuss the most effective way of dealing with this in Chapter 5.

3   Do you see your child as evil?
When you have reached the end of the line and are ready to swing for your child, you may believe that he has the devil in him and that nothing more can be done. Should you believe this, though, it is important for you to realise that you are *feeling* and not thinking here. In Chapter 2 we looked at various aspects of bullying in an attempt to take an objective view of the matter. Unless you are able to do this, you are not in a position to help your child.

Because you are still reading this book I presume that you still have a hope that he may redeem himself. You are reading it because you feel that you may be able to help him. Should any of us truly believe in the possibility of children being evil at birth, we might well despair and let the devil rule. No child is born evil, of course, and all are capable of being nurtured to maturity.

What we must recognise is that when they are born they all have different needs. Earlier we discussed the underlying fragility or resilience found in each human being, and how his interplays with their self-esteem. We saw how defence mechanisms operate to maintain a consistent self-image. When you think of your child you should see him in these terms; if you project the image of the devil on to him, you must remember that he may assume this form!

Your attitude to your victim
1 Do you see your child as weak and feeble?
If you perceive her in this way it may be that she has none of the qualities of your ideal model. You may have had a picture in your mind of what you wanted her to be before she was born. Perhaps you wanted her to be different from you—the implication of this is that there are many things that you do not like about your own personality. But concentrate, no matter how hard it is for you, on seeing the good things about yourself and on recognising the positive strengths of your child. If you can begin to see your own good qualities, you will be able to see hers.

If you simply cannot relate the two, perhaps you are too much of a bully or a victim yourself.

To help you sort out these issues it would help if you were to work out your personal definition of strength and weakness. Remember that a strong person does not necessarily have physical strength, and besides, there are many big softies. Personal strength comes from a healthy belief in oneself. A weak person is one who has no conviction of his worth.

If you feel that you have a weak personality, do all you can to enhance your feeling of personal identity. As a parent, don't be afraid to separate psychologically from your family. You should see your own personal interests and hobbies as being an essential part of your identity. When your child thinks of you she will think of what you do and what your interests are.

If you have your own commitments and convictions you will find that you no longer try to live through your child, and that you are providing her with a worthwhile model. Strike out and make more of a life of your own, and you will have less time to pamper her: and she may have time to grow and become more independent.

If, on the other hand, you feel that you have a str

personality and that you are domineering, consider others more. Listen rather than talk. When you talk, listen to yourself: do you speak only of your affairs, or are you asking others about their lives and feelings? Check how much you use the techniques mentioned in the discussion of defence mechanisms (p. 58).

2 Do you see your child as withdrawn?

If she appears to be too much inside herself, do not urge her to be more active. Recognise that she may have retreated for a while into the safety of her own world. When she is ready, she will emerge. You can help by making the world outside appealing to her. This does not mean that you will always be arranging exciting things for her to do, or that you will be constantly taking cream cakes into her room. You must be careful not to reinforce her behaviour in this way.

Be careful, too, not to place her under any degree of pressure. She already has enough on her mind. You can make the world outside seem attractive by simply being there and not questioning. If you become anxious about her being withdrawn, you may encourage her behaviour. There are times when all of us need solitude, and the assumption that everyone should be gregarious may be questioned.

If you do look upon your child as withdrawn you should again be aware that it may be a question of her not fulfilling your expectations. Indeed, this might be the very reason why she has decided to retreat.

3 Do you see your child as a waste of time?

Maybe you have reached the point where you have given up. It seems impossible to get her interested in anything. She seems to have no enthusiasm for life, no get-up-and-go. No mettle.

There is really only one thing you can do about this: go and look in the mirror. If you see yourself there and nobody else, then recognise the realities of life. Your face is different from any other; your personality is unique. Look at your child in the same way, and give her credit where credit is due. More importantly, you should realise that it is wrong to assume that you can impose your life on to hers.

If you say that your child is a waste of time, you have given up. Look back in the mirror: do you see her staring at you? If you want to see a vibrant, enthusiastic child, develop your own enthusiasm for life. As long as you do not *demand* that she share it, you will most likely find her following in your footsteps.

PROMOTING AGGRESSIVE BEHAVIOUR

Playgroups

Playgroups and nursery schools can promote aggression as well as control it. They can also cause children to be withdrawn. Much aggressive behaviour goes unnoticed by supervisors, and passive children are encouraged to be more assertive. In general, though, children attending playgroups exhibit few problems, and as we have already noted there is good evidence that they stand less of a chance of developing into antisocial characters later in life.

So parents who, because of their work, must send their child to playgroup, should be considerably consoled. It is in the playgroup that the child develops his skills of negotiating and generally coping with other children. This is invaluable, and can prevent early failure when he starts school. The child who may tend to bully and the child who may be withdrawn and timid both benefit by attending playgroup, providing there is adequate trained supervision. However, their tendencies will be promoted, if they are ignored. Supervisors should be skilled at helping children to learn how to cope with each other and how to curb their less acceptable natural impulses.

If you send your child to a playgroup, seek reassurance on the qualifications and training of those in charge. Satisfy yourself that the staff–child ratio is good enough for effective supervision to take place.

Aggressive games

Children who are excessively aggressive will have their behaviour reinforced if they are exposed to violent games. While others harmlessly experience horror through the fantasy of play, the aggressive child has her lifestyle condoned.

If a child is considered to be excessively aggressive or passive she should not take part in aggressive play. If she does, her condition will worsen.

If you have a child whom you consider to be excessively aggressive, do not presume that by allowing her to release her energies you are going to calm her down. Although she may in the short term appear to have settled, this will not last for long, and by allowing her to be aggressive you will be promoting her condition. If, on the other hand, you have a child who is withdrawn and timid you would do nothing for her self-image if you were to insist that she take part in aggressive games. Rather than toughening her up as you might hope, she would become even more passive.

Television and films
Aggressive children who repeatedly watch violence on TV or in films will become more violent. If a bully sees a bully on TV he will have his self-image condoned: he will identify with violent antisocial characters. Passive children may become more passive by being allowed to watch as much TV as they want to.

When you are deciding which programmes you want your child to view, bear in mind the way in which we all identify with characters who have the same traits as ourselves. If your child is aggressive and domineering he should not watch violent and aggressive films. This may be difficult, since most parents find that the only way of getting some peace is to sit their child in front of a television. If you find that you can do nothing else to occupy him, rent suitable videos and control his viewing—and limit the viewing times of your passive child.

Competitive sport
Involvement in aggressive, competitive sport only encourages aggression. The hope that it will *release* aggression in a cathartic way is not supported. When aggressive children are taken to the swimming-pool to let off steam, their aggression level increases. So if you have a child whom you consider to be excessively aggressive, do not try to make him into a boxer: he may end up committing murder! Highly

aggressive children are also impulsive. Top sportsmen undoubtedly need a great deal of aggression if they are to succeed, but they also need to be disciplined and in full control of their emotions.

The passive, withdrawn child may of course suffer unduly when he is forced to take part in open competition—especially where an element of aggression is required. He will feel embarrassed and humiliated, and his self-esteem will plummet.

In general terms, children should be encouraged to take part in sport to improve performance—that is, their own—and help others to do the same. They should measure their success against themselves. Regrettably, though, much sport resembles tribal warfare. The ultimate accolade, to represent your country, satisfies the need to belong but at the same time promotes a less desirable primitive instinct. Aggressive, bullying children can only identify with the latter. In their minds it is all about annihilating the opposition.

Triggers for anger
It is important to avoid outbursts of aggression. When a child has an outburst she lets herself down considerably. The longer she can go without one, the more will her positive behaviour be reinforced. There are three main reasons why a child reacts aggressively, and you may trigger her aggression if you are not aware of them:

1 when she feels that her objectives are being thwarted;
2 when anyone criticises her or her friends;
3 when she feels that a situation is unjust or that someone has been negligent or careless.

If you are to avoid your child becoming upset, make sure that objectives are realistic and within her reach; be wary of saying anything that could be construed as criticism; always explain everything to her clearly and precisely, and be consistent in your approach. We discussed earlier how aggression is based on frustration and threat. If you feel that you have a fragile child you must do all you can to avoid her feeling frustrated and vulnerable. A clue to success is clear communication, which we shall be discussing in Chapter 5

We shall also be discussing the need for you to control
your child, and the way in which your parenting style can
make her into a bully or a victim.

CONCLUSION

I hope that this chapter has provided you with an insight
into the needs of your child and that you can now better
appreciate the relationship you have with her. In describing
how you should look at this, I have not meant to imply that
everything is your fault and that the responsibility for her
behaviour rests only with you. Your child is the essential
part of the equation and has a responsibility of her own; you
and others can only try to provide the optimum setting for
her to be able to assume this responsibility.

Neither have I intended to give the impression that you
must only understand your child for everything to work.
Your understanding is necessary, but I am sure that you will
agree that it is not enough. It needs to be accompanied by
action. We shall be looking at what may be done, and by
whom, in Part Two.

In the final chapter of preparation, before we set about
actually tackling the issue, we shall look at the needs of
children, of their parents and of the professionals who work
with them. By doing so we may finally begin to put the
complex problem of bullying into perspective.

HAROLD BRIDGES LIBRARY
S. MARTIN'S COLLEGE
LANCASTER

5 Everyone's Needs

When we think of bullies and victims we have a tendency to imagine that they are somehow separate and different from the rest of us. In one sense they are.

But they do not exist in a vacuum. They are part of society and their personalities are intrinsically linked with those around them. We feel that they are different because they are at the end of the spectrum; in their excessive aggressiveness or passivity, their reactions are extreme. They therefore have the same needs as everyone else, but the difference is that theirs are greater.

Those who care for them must be more consciously aware of what these needs are. When you are dealing with children who present you with few difficulties, there is no reason to make a conscious effort to understand their behaviour. They are resilient enough to be able to cope with any setbacks, and they even benefit from the strengthening aspect of developmental stress. Bullies and victims, however, should be viewed as children who are born with specific traits that make them more vulnerable to environmental pressures. They need special attention, if the consequences of their natural tendencies are to be managed.

THE NEEDS OF ALL CHILDREN

Navigation skills

1 The need to have a clear picture of the world
A child needs to know that certain things will always happen and that certain people will always be there. He needs to know where he stands in relation to everything around him. He needs a map of his personal world, one which he can recognise and read and one where the compass points do not change. If there is nobody in charge to provide him with

rules and boundaries for his behaviour, he will feel lost and uncared for.

But if somebody provides him with a behaviour map, he will learn to use it. Later he will be able to apply the rules of navigation to new scenarios, his safety being assured by the Bay of Knowledge to which he may always return.

2   The need to have an objective in life

A child needs to have a level of expectation to work to. He needs to sense that there is something for him to achieve, and that this objective is in the interests of others and not just of himself. If he has been provided with a behaviour map he will *know* that there are things to achieve. Equipped with some basic skills in navigation, he will travel as far as his innate curiosity and ingenuity can take him.

But if the picture of his world is confused and blurred he will remain in harbour, his natural impulses frustrated and latently problematic.

3   The need to feel part of things

A child needs to feel a sense of relatedness, to be able to see herself as part of a whole. She needs to sense that she is of value to others, that she is part of a network of relationships, a network that gives her a sense of her identity. She needs to belong.

If she cannot sense where she belongs there is no hope that she will ever go anywhere. She will remain in irons, unable to see the shoreline and frightened to venture into uncharted waters.

4   The need for stimulation

A child needs stimulation. This will help to develop her language and her capacity for abstract thought. It will also help her to develop her inner controls. But if she is confined to harbour because of her inability to make sense of the map that has been provided or because there is little wind to take her elsewhere, she will become bored. She may decide to fire a salvo at the harbourmaster, or even sink her own ship—just to make her mark.

5   The need for a sense of rootedness

A child needs to bond with his mother. This happens in the very early stages of childhood and provides him with the basis for his future development. From this he can emerge as a separate person with a sense of independence, free will and control. If the bonding does *not* take place with his mother or another significant person, he may later attempt to form a similar relationship with others and either try to control them (sadism) or be controlled by them (masochism). He may become excessively fond of himself or have a craving to destroy.

Thus, to continue our analogy, if the child has no anchor point he may drift into dangerous waters, and may grasp at tenuous safety lines. In his confusion he may attempt to capture another ship, or alternatively he may give his vessel away.

6   The need for love

The sense of love, of unconditional acceptance, is built into the bonding process between a child and his mother; we also believe that it can be achieved in a slightly different form with others. Unconditional acceptance is not the only necessary component—it is just as important to recognise that love means caring, and that caring means trying to provide all the needs that we have already mentioned.

If these needs are not met, we have the picture of a child lost at sea. He does not know where he has come from, or where he wants to go. Even if he did have an ultimate destination, he would not have the skill to get there. He can only become confused, and in his frustration will either strike out at others or turn his aggression on himself. A child who is particularly vulnerable will need considerable assistance if he is to navigate successfully towards maturity.

Communication and negotiation skills

1   Speaking

Children need to be able to communicate with each other and with parents. Before they are able to speak they develop a capacity to interpret language and to assess a person's intentions. As they grow, they listen to their parents and absorb their vocabulary and speech mechanisms. They then use these in conjunction with an innate capacity to generate their own language. Speaking helps them to make sense of the world around them; as they speak they label objects, as well as assigning words to things that they can only feel and not touch. Parents who encourage their children to speak, by asking them questions, are helping them to think and to create a map of their personal world.

You should realise, though, that one of the benefits of language is that it enables children not only to communicate but to negotiate. If the central purpose of teaching your child how to communicate is only for her to express her thoughts and wishes freely, you could be promoting an ego-centric and domineering bully. Encourage her to understand that there are other people in the world, and show her how to negotiate with them.

2   Non-verbal communication
Using words is not the only way for a child to express herself. Most children begin by drawing pictures and playing with toys. They may dress up and act out their thoughts and feelings. They may curl their body up into the shape of an orange, or gather their thoughts into a tray of sand.

You should not insist that a child talks to you or that she writes down her thoughts and feelings. The latter in particular can often best be expressed in drawing, modelling, acting or computing. In every home and classroom there should be materials and equipment for the child to use in this way. This kind of activity is vital to her, no matter what her age. It enables her to get in touch with herself and thereafter with others.

If your child can be helped to express herself like this she may, with your gentle assistance, be led into verbal inter-action. During activity sessions, whether she is a five-year-old doing her clay modelling or a teenager on her computer, you can begin to talk to her about what she is doing. This will be her first step towards being able to articulate her feelings and thereafter to control her emotions.

3 Modelling

Whether you are a parent or a professional you should always bear in mind the tendency of your child to model herself on those around her. If you do not take pride in your appearance, self-care and presentation will not be important to her. If you treat those around you aggressively, she will think this is the way to behave. All children model themselves in this way on adults who are significant to them.

You should therefore clearly express your own thoughts and feelings about your concern for others. Your child will probably model herself on you; she will be able to express herself clearly and will consider the welfare of others.

If you are loud and domineering and do not listen to what others have to say, she will also be like this. If you are quiet and mutter your thoughts, she will reflect this in her confused thinking and lack of a sense of direction.

When you talk to her, balance your inclination to come down to her level with her need to listen to adult speech. If you do nothing but gurgle at her until she is three, you can guarantee that her speech will be three years behind where it should be. It is also important for parents and professionals who work with older children to realise that they make themselves look foolish in the children's eyes when they relate to them as thought they were the same age. Adolescents often adopt their own group language patterns, and they will not accept an older person if he attempts to intrude. We must maintain a generation gap (see p. 60).

4 Detecting subtexts

When children can communicate effectively, their messages are straightforward and without complication. But if a child is vulnerable his language and actions may be loaded with hidden meanings—subtexts—because he is speaking to you through a filter of emotions.

When you speak to your vulnerable child bear in mind that he may also be misinterpreting what you are saying. It may be necessary for you to speak slowly and to repeat what you have to say in a number of different ways. If he reacts passively or aggressively to what you say, remain consistent; do not alter course. The subtext of his negative response is his reluctance to accept what you have said. It takes time for him to do this. You will find that if you maintain your position he will comply.

Be careful, though, not to respond in a firm way that is also aggressive (we have already mentioned how this can only escalate the problem). He will win any battle when it comes to an emotional interchange, so show your resolve by being firm but calm. It would be a good idea to gently try to help him to say exactly what he means, but don't hurry it. When he is strong enough, it will happen.

Practise looking for subtexts. If you can decode his language in this way you will be in a position to meet his needs. When you are dealing with him, look at the way his body speaks to you. As with all of us he has little control over it. If he continually appears to half-turn away from you when you speak to him, it will be because it hurts him too much to acknowledge what you are saying; if he sprawls across his chair when he is speaking to you in a meaningful, rational way, you may assume that he has ambivalent feelings about what he is saying.

5 Listening

If you are listening carefully you will hear the child's subtexts. He may begin to tell you how he feels about himself and his problems. Allow him to do this. But do not be tempted to prod and probe into his past; be wary of putting words into his mouth, and do not start telling him how he should behave and why things went wrong for him. You are there to listen—not to teach or talk, or to satisfy your curiosity. A great deal of harm can be done by adults projecting their own interpretations into children's minds.

They may also tend to believe in the urgency of a child looking into his past; believing that they may thereby relieve him of his problems, they often begin by digging at the foundations of his personality before he has built up enough strength to remain standing. Adults recognise feelings and dynamics that children cannot; by projecting these into a child's mind they provide him with psychological and behavioural models that have no basis in either his intellect or his emotions.

Consistency

Children need to have a consistent picture of their world (p. 69). This is created for them by significant adults who have assumed their status because of their own consistency. When a child thinks of them, it is of them as representing something. They mean something to her in terms, for instance, of their physical make-up and the way they dress. In her mind she may hear their unique accent or a phrase that they regularly use. She may associate them with their hobbies or their work. They remain consistent in her mind, and she adopts their style and values.

We have already mentioned the need to consider the perception your child has of you. If you are inconsistent in your dealings with her, being firm at one moment and giving in at the next, she will see you as weak and unreliable. She will not respect you. Neither will she respect you if you are consistent only in that you stand for nothing or that you never expect anything from her. If she is naturally aggressive, she will assume a belligerent stance and bounce against everyone in an attempt to feel a sense of identity. If she is naturally passive, she will give up as she recognises that there is no one who cares anyway.

When you are trying to be consistent, bear in mind the harm you could do by being too domineering. If you have a child who tends to be aggressive, she will react defensively and the situation will escalate; if your child is passive, she will retreat even more into her shell. You must be aware that both kinds of children use their defence mechanisms in this way; they are very sensitive to any threat to their personality. They will always react like this if they sense that *you* are on the defensive, and to avoid it happening you will need to be clear about what you want from your child.

When you are considering your requirements, make sure that you know why you are asking her to behave in any particular way; make sure also that success is within her reach. When you express yourself, believe in the fairness of what you are saying and remain firm and calm.

Parents usually come in pairs, and should of course have agreed on their approach beforehand. Each parent is an individual, and will have his or her own relationship with the child. To avoid problem behaviour, they too need to communicate and negotiate; only by doing this will they be able to project consistent boundaries for the child's behaviour.

Rewards and punishments

When parents or professionals are dealing with difficult children they have a tendency to focus on unwanted behaviour and pay attention to a child only when he is misbehaving.

Rather than taking this approach, you should look for occasions when you can reinforce your child's acceptable behaviour. When he is playing quietly on his computer or amusing himself by drawing, do not feel that you should leave him while he is settled. These are the times when you should offer the occasional favourable comment or interested question, or refreshments such as a drink or a sandwich.

Do not say why you are doing this: allow your child to associate the pleasure he experiences from your reward with his acceptable behaviour. If you make it obvious what you are doing it will become a game for him and be ineffective in terms of altering his behaviour.

Whenever you can, introduce rewards that involve sharing an activity with your child, such as going swimming together or watching a video. In this way you will build a relationship with him which will result in him responding positively to your controls.

Some children can be told; others have to be told and shown. Those who are vulnerable have not only to be told and shown, they also have to be helped to appreciate the consequences of their behaviour. Although you should focus on rewarding your child's acceptable behaviour, if you are dealing with a difficult child you will undoubtedly need to reinforce your words with sanctions, and it is important to work out what these might be. Prepare a list of sanctions based on your child's interests and motivations, varied and graded according to severity.

Some popular and effective ideas for sanctions are extra chores around the house, going early to bed, the suspension of privileges or the withdrawal of leisure activities. Some sanctions are illegal and these are listed in Appendix A.

Controls

Children need to have someone controlling their lives. If they sense that there is no one in charge, they feel lost and their behaviour deteriorates.

Parents sometimes mistakenly believe that to encourage their child to be creative and spontaneous they need to release her from all rules and regulations. Invariably, the child lacks the motivation and self-discipline to put any talent she may have to good use. The parents usually base their belief on the outrageous assumption that creative geniuses do not need self-discipline and control.

All children need external controls, and through these they progress to the point where they adjust the rules that they have internalised to meet their own requirements. Thus their creativity can have some meaning for others.

On the other hand, children who are over-controlled can become passive; usually this happens because they have given up any hope of meeting the unrealistic expectations of their parents. They assume a negative identity, and are alienated from their parents and from the world around them.

Achieving the right balance of control is a matter of preparing yourself before you walk the tightrope.

Discipline

Parents tend to react to situations in the same way as their own parents did. As they grow older they become more and more like them in many ways, but they are not always fully aware of it. When it comes to disciplining their children, for instance, they usually do whatever their parents did to them. Thus it is that those parents who were provided with few controls provide few for their children, and those who were dominated or abused tend to abuse.

There is therefore a great need to examine how you discipline your child. You must be able to stand back and be objective about your approach, and not slip into the way of simply imagining that you are doing things differently. Listen to yourself speak to your child: do you remind yourself of your father or mother? Do you react in the same way and dole out the same old punishments, or have you really been able to break out of this vicious circle?

If you have a child who presents no difficulties you have little to be concerned about in this respect, but if your child is a potential bully or victim you need to make every effort to break a cycle of behaviour that can so easily pass from one generation to the next. If you can do this you will have achieved something remarkable: you will have had the courage to look at yourself and to make a conscious change, and in doing so you will be affecting the lives of your son and of his offspring.

When you are looking at your approach, consider the following:

1   Does the amount of discipline you administer depend on your mood, or does it depend on your child's behaviour?
If you discipline your child only when you are in a bad mood, you are using him as a whipping-boy on whom to vent your own frustration. Consistency is an essential part of discipline—without it, discipline becomes abuse.

2   Are you able to present your child with clear decisions?
Many parents give confused messages to their children. If you want your discipline to be effective it has to be consistent (p. 75) and uniformly applied. You will need to negotiate with your partner on the rules that can never be violated, and those less important ones that may be adjusted. This can be done to great effect as a special, unexpected and rare treat.

3   Do you share any activities with your child?
He will only accept discipline if you have shared enjoyable experiences with him. Make every effort to do things together. If you are unable to do sport, play chess; if you are unable to play chess with him, share a video.

You may say that this is not what he wants: when you suggest it, he becomes antagonistic and aggressive. The key to success in this respect is always to take an objective approach. Do not say that you are going to share a video with him and that you hope he enjoys being with you. He is likely to walk out. Be more subtle. Rent a video which you know will appeal to him, let him know it is there but do not say it is for him, and when he watches it, quietly join him. Do the same thing at the same time the next week. Repeat ad infinitum. He may gradually be able to talk to you about something that you have in common, that you have shared. You will be able to discuss the merits of Tom and Gerry and set them against the Road Runner. (You must be prepared to sacrifice something!) After a while, you will find that he responds much better when you ask him to clear his socks from under the bed.

Do not expect immediate change with any technique that you employ; give everything a good try before you turn to something else. Above all else, use your imagination and be subtle!

Freedom

We have talked a lot about controls, and now we must discuss the need that your child has for freedom.

When she is young she will need time to be on her own, to play and to explore. You must allow this, and only be there when other children are likely to cause her difficulty.

As she grows, she will benefit from having her own room, to which she can retreat whenever she needs. If she tends to be withdrawn and to use her room too much, define the times when she can be there. Gradually reduce the time allowed, but never curtail it altogether, nor deny her access as punishment. Always leave her with a way out. If she has nowhere to go to escape any pressure she may feel, you will be faced with a reaction.

When your child is aggressive, it is in her room that she can cool off. Encourage her to use it in this way. If there are things for her to do rather than just things for her to smash up, she will be able to avoid letting herself down when she feels ready to explode. In providing this facility, again, you must use subtlety: supply the attractive setting, but do not blackmail her with it. Do not say that you are providing all this at great expense and sacrifice just to help her. If you do, when she needs to have a shot at you she will expend her emotions on the room.

Provide whatever you can afford to put in it. It would be a good idea to invite her to choose the wallpaper, for instance, thereby allowing her to feel that the room really is her own. Remember to be consistent. If you need access, arrange details beforehand. If she is not allowed to play music before eight o'clock in the morning, make this clear from the beginning.

As your child enters adolescence she has an increasing need to be herself. She has reached the point where she needs to be in charge of her own life (Chapter 3). She also needs the freedom to think: she no longer wishes to accept the values of someone else, least of all her parents. She needs the freedom to determine whether she will pray or not; she needs to decide when she will play and when she will work.

Freedom becomes increasingly important to a child as she grows. However, she cannot cope with freedom if you have failed to provide her with external controls in her developing years. It will be your controls that she relies on, long after you have gone your separate ways.

THE NEEDS OF PARENTS AND PROFESSIONALS

Parents have as many needs as children. If they were born with a sensitive, fragile personality or a tendency to react aggressively, they may have experienced many difficulties in their lives; their greatest need is to be understood and supported.

Regrettably, the opposite usually occurs. They are made to feel entirely responsible for the behaviour of their child. They are often called into school to explain his behaviour, and made to feel entirely responsible for him. No parent wants her child to behave poorly, and it is even less likely that she wants him to be a bully or a victim. Yet when bullying or victimising or any other undesirable behaviour occurs it is the parent who is blamed.

Professionals should realise that we only blame when we do not know what to do about something.

Parents do, of course, have a tremendous influence on the way their child behaves. Throughout Part One we have been looking at how they might examine their approach, but we have not been apportioning blame. We have been trying to understand the part that parents play in order that we may be sympathetic to their needs. If you are a teacher or child care worker, I do hope you have read Part One for this purpose. Unless you stop blaming parents and begin to understand the complexity of their responsibilities, you will not be able to provide them with the support they so badly need.

Parents of difficult children need:

1   a listening ear;
2   suggestions, when they ask for them;
3   support in a common approach to their child.

Should professionals be able to provide the first of these without judgemental interjections, they may find that the behaviour of the child concerned alters quite dramatically. If they can offer suggestions when they are requested rather than make more demands on parents who are already harassed by their children, together they may be able to decide upon an approach that will be effective—and effective largely because it will have been mutually agreed and implemented.

MORE SPECIFIC NEEDS

Bullies

I do hope that by this stage you are in a frame of mind to be serious about the needs of bullies! The most common and instinctive reaction is to say that they need a taste of their own medicine. But if you were to say this you would be putting the cart before the horse. We need to establish their needs clearly before we can meet them:

1   They need to become less impulsive; their behaviour needs to be inhibited.
2   Their desire for power and dominance over others needs to be diminished.
3   They need to be less hostile to the world around them.
4   They need to appreciate why it is wrong to bully.

5 They need to empathise with their victim.
6 They need to be able to take responsibility for their actions.

Passive victims
You will most likely be more sympathetic to the idea that victims need help:

1 They need to be less anxious and to feel more secure.
2 They need to be less cautious and not so quiet and sensitive.
3 They need to improve their self-esteem.
4 They need to develop more friendships.
5 They need to have a more aggressive approach to life.

Provocative victims
Provocative victims have the same needs as the passive victim. In addition:

1 They need to be more focused—restful and on task.
2 They need to be less immature.
3 They need to stop irritating others and creating tension.

Special Needs
Children with Special Needs are more likely to be involved in bullying. Their particular characteristics are used by bullies as an excuse for harassment. The child who has learning difficulties or a physical handicap is usually more isolated than others and has fewer friends: he is therefore more vulnerable than most to the attentions of the bully. Also, his own fragility means that he has a heightened sensitivity and that he will over-react if he feels threatened: in secondary schools, boys with Special Needs are more likely to bully than others.

Generally, at the secondary stage there is less of a decrease in bullying among children with Special Needs than there is among others. Another difference is that, among children with Special Needs, girls in junior/middle schools bully as much as boys. So such children must be given special consideration in terms of their relatively high involvement in bullying.

CONCLUSION

We all have needs, and I am sure you would subscribe to the view that some of us have greater needs than others! If you are to be personally involved in tackling bullying, you must be honest about your own needs and, especially, about the relationship and attitude you have to both the bully and the victim.

If you are a professional it is vital that you develop a working relationship with parents, and to do this you must appreciate the stress under which difficult children place them. Bear in mind that parents have to live day in, day out, with the children who create such problems for you, whereas you have to put up with them only during your working shift. And besides, you know, don't you, that ultimately they are not really your responsibility!?

Do not blame the parents for their child's behaviour; we all enter life in unique circumstances, with both strengths and weaknesses. None of us wishes to fail. Professionals should ask themselves whether they could tolerate the thought of their own child being a bully or a victim. If they could not, how much worse must it be for a person who may well be less resilient than themselves?

Noting the needs of bullies does not imply that we are condoning their behaviour. Describing the needs of a victim does not imply that we are disparaging or condemning him.

You have now completed the preparation stage, so take time to review what you have read.

There may be many issues that you still need to resolve. In Part Two we will begin to examine how we might manage the bully and the victim, and how we might deal with their behaviour in both the home and at school. Do remember that, despite what anyone may suggest, as his or her parent you are the one who is going to have to deal with the problem. It is essential, therefore, for you to pause now and assess your thoughts. A good way to do this would be to jot down two or three questions which have occurred to you from each chapter and invite your friend from Chapter 1 to come for a coffee, or go for a drink. If you cannot think of any questions of your own, take another look at those you tried to answer in Chapter 3 and see whether matters have become any clearer to you.

Part Two

TACKLING THE PROBLEM

6 Managing the Bully

You began in Chapter 1 by asking yourself some questions about your child's behaviour: you will remember that the purpose of the exercises you undertook was not necessarily to help you towards a conclusion about whether he is a bully or not, but to define more precisely those parts of his behaviour that were giving you cause for concern.

A great deal of anxiety can be avoided if the child's actual behaviour is analysed. When it is, a parent may suddenly find, for example, that the root cause of her anxiety is the fact that she cannot get him to clear his room of dirty linen; or the teacher may suddenly discover that colouring everything is her annoyance at the way the child speaks to her. Both parent and professional often promote unacceptable behaviour from a bedrock of anxiety arising from such matters; a small problem gradually promotes a negative level of expectation in relation to the child's behaviour. Nothing is expected but trouble: by the time he is involved in bullying, the original cause of anxiety is forgotten.

It is often necessary for professionals to re-focus on individual children rather than on the group—at least, to begin with. But they often become anxious about tackling the bully directly and prefer to deal with the issue in a roundabout way. This is far more comfortable for them, and avoids possible embarrassment. However, although it is vital to have a group policy on bullying at the class level and at the whole-school level (see Chapter 10), it is of critical importance for adults to deal directly and immediately with incidents of bullying or suspected bullying. In this way they may nip the problem in the bud. One of the golden rules when dealing with children is: if you shout about the little things, the big things will never happen. (Incidentally, a companion rule to this one is that if you shout too much, they will never hear you!)

Part One was all about the essential business of preparation, of looking at yourself and developing an approach in broad terms. We will press on now with practical matters.

I am sure that you are reading this book because you are keen to know what you might do about a specific child who is causing you problems. Not knowing the details of his behaviour or his age, I must frame my comments in general terms, relying on you to select those suggestions that are appropriate for your child, or to replace them with similar suitable exercises. In Chapter 8 we will be discussing ways of dealing with actual bullying episodes; in this chapter and the next we will consider how the needs of the bully and of the victim may be met in both the home and the school.

HIS IMPULSIVE AND UNINHIBITED BEHAVIOUR

Your aim should be to provide your child with a controlling environment.

A controlling environment is one where there are rules and regulations that determine a child's behaviour. He does not do what he immediately feels like: he stops to think whether he is allowed to behave in this way. He then proceeds. If he breaks the rules and nothing happens, then the rules cease to exist for him. If he abides by the rules and receives no praise, they have been weakened as far as he is concerned; if he abides by the rules and is praised for doing so, he will begin to make those rules his own. He will internalise them, and in future will be able to apply them in the absence of a controlling person; and he will be able to apply them to an endless variety of unique situations.

AT HOME
You will need to be subtle to be effective in your approach. Do not start by making a list of rules and insisting that they be obeyed—I have a feeling that your child would tell you what to do with them! What you are aiming to do is gradually to introduce the structure that has somehow disappeared, or that was never there to the extent that it should have been. Your requirements should centre on:

Times: getting up, going to bed, meals, watching television, homework.

Chores: washing up, taking rubbish out, putting milk bottles on doorstep, cleaning car, taking dog for walk.

Personal: cleaning teeth, cleaning shoes, dressing, placing dirty clothes in linen basket.

Events (weekly): Friday night is cinema night; Monday means Youth Club.

I am sure that you will be able to make a far more effective and interesting list than this!

Prioritise
Start by making four private lists:

1   five things he does well in the home;
2   three things you would like him to change, in order of priority (make sure that these are within his reach—you could be cornered into a no-win situation if you get this wrong!);
3   six things he would like as a reward, in order of priority;
4   six effective sanctions, in order of potency.

State your requirements
Choose item 3 (the least important) from list 2. (It is important to start with an item of lesser importance in order that your child has the greatest chance of success.)

Talk to your child in private
1   Calmly explain your requirements to him, very specifically and precisely.
2   Tell him that he will be punished if he does not comply. (Do not tell him how he will be punished: he may think the punishment worthwhile!)
3   Tell him that you care for him and that you want you both to be able to get on together, but that you insist that he meet these requirements.

Consolidate
If your child complies:

1 Praise and reward judiciously. (Use list 3.)
2 When you feel that the new rule has been established, select the second item on list 2 and repeat the process.
3 Continue to praise him for further success with the first rule.
4 After further consolidation, choose item 3 on list 2 and repeat the process.
5 When all three items of behaviour have been adjusted, make a new set of requirements and repeat.
6 Keep praising him for continued success with the original set of requirements.

Punish
If your child fails to comply, face him with the weakest of the items from your list of sanctions. If he still does not comply, work your way through the sanctions list (to the top, if necessary). If he refuses to cooperate, it may be because your requirements are not within his reach. It may also be that he is playing around with you. You must carefully judge the situation and, being aware of any prejudices you may have, decide whether you are going to reassess the target behaviour.

It *could* be disastrous if you had to change course. So make every effort, in advance, to assess his ability to meet your requirements, especially the first one you put to him. Make sure, too, that you comply with all legal requirements regarding the punishment of children (Appendix A).

Review
If you are effectively to implement a programme such as this, it may take many months. You should not, though, drift endlessly on pursuing each target. Give yourself a month, and as you approach the end of it assess your success. Decide whether to swap your target for another, and how you are going to do this.

If you regularly assess the state of affairs you will be able to adjust and change, and remain in control. If you fail to assess his behaviour, you may feel that things have got better when in reality they have got worse.

If you persist in this way, the structure missing from your child's life may gradually be introduced. His impulsivity can, in the short term, be curbed only by the controlling forces around him. The stronger they are, the more inhibited will be his unacceptable behaviour.

AT SCHOOL

In Chapter 10 we shall be dealing more fully with the way in which schools as a whole and classroom teachers might produce a more controlling environment. A general rule that individual teachers might note is that the more freedom an aggressive child has, the more aggressive he will become.

In addition to the need to adhere to the normal daily timetable, the bully should be given:

1   duties and responsibilities during breaktimes;
2   duties and responsibilities at lunchtimes;
3   classroom duties and responsibilities.

It is necessary that these privileges be installed not only in order that they may have a controlling effect—in that they are to be seen as responsibilities—but that they may be used as sanctions and withdrawn. The more goodies you are able to give, the more you can take away.

Teachers may balk at the thought of presenting a bully with such an opportunity to exert power. As with all behaviour modification, its effectiveness depends on timing. When you, the teacher, first receive your class, and usually before, you know which children are going to cause difficulty. But they do not know that you know, so you can give them all a fresh start and award as many privileges and responsibilities as you wish. My suggestion is that you give them to the bully. Imposing a pro-social image may just work, and in any case it should last long enough for the bully to want to retain his privileged position. When you have to remove his new status, he may resent it. Thus you have your control . . . Clearly, the message is that you should find out as much about your new class as possible before it arrives.

The same processes for behaviour modification as recommended for parents (p. 76) can be implemented *vis-à-vis* individual bullies in schools. Many teachers become concerned about the difficulty of consistently applying such a programme throughout the school day. In junior schools children remain with their class teacher for much of the time, whereas in secondary schools it is more difficult because they have different teachers for different subjects. In practice, when such a programme is being implemented it is sensible, anyway, to limit it to specific times of the day when it can be consistently monitored, and not to worry about trying to get a reading from across the board. Report cards passed from teacher to teacher usually become meaningless because of the inevitable variation in the level of staff commitment to the programme and because of the unreliability of such a subjective approach. They tend to do more harm than good, serving only to assuage the bully's guilt.

In providing a controlled environment the teacher must be aware, as must the parent, that he may, by the heavy imposition of rules and by too harsh a condemnation of certain pupils, be projecting himself as a bully. The fact is that teachers often bully and are unaware of it. Their demeanour and style may be intimidating to those much younger than themselves; they may not make a conscious effort to resist the cynical remark or the pointed comment. Many do not look upon the behaviour of the children in their classes as their concern. Should a child behave badly, the teacher invariably rejects him, regarding him as a complication in an otherwise more or less smooth day. Teachers often imagine that they are in the classroom only to teach their subjects; rarely are they, nor do they look upon themselves as, specialists in child development and behaviour. But if they were to focus on the precise needs of each child in this respect, and if they were more aware of the effect they, as individuals, have on the children, they would become far more successful teachers.

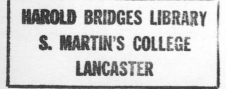

HAROLD BRIDGES LIBRARY
S. MARTIN'S COLLEGE
LANCASTER

HIS DESIRE FOR POWER AND DOMINANCE

Your aim should be to strengthen those around him. Bully-ing can be seen as the result of an imbalance. If the forces that prevail around a bully are strong, he will not bully. He only does so when he senses weakness.

AT HOME:
You may well be a healthily assertive parent, but if for any reason you are not, the following advice may help.

Assess what you mean to him, or to anyone else
1 What do you do in your spare time?
2 What are your political views?
3 What is your main ambition in life?

Take action
1 Make sure that you have an interest in something. Take a night class; join a society. If you cannot afford to do this, you can still have a hobby. Walking is good for you, and a well respected activity; and gardening and bird-watching are popular enthusiasms. Research your interest free of charge at your library. When you are there look on the notice board—you may find that a group of enthusiasts meets near you.
  Pondering on things in your armchair in front of the tele-vision is not good enough. Children do not respect couch potatoes. You must do something. Physical exercise is extremely good for you, since it will strengthen you not just physically but psychologically.

2 You must have views on politics or on the rights and wrongs of what is going on around you. If you don't already, start by buying a national newspaper and looking at current issues; use your local library to become better acquainted with popular topics. Do not keep your views to yourself: practise stating your opinion, but do still listen to others. You may find that if you let your views be known it will bring you friends who have similar thoughts and interests.

3 You must have dreams and aspirations. If you are like

many people, you will never have told others what they are. Try discussing them light-heartedly, and try sharing with others your fears and apprehensions. It is by doing this that you will become close to them.

It is important that you mean something to those around you, that in their eyes you stand for something. If you can achieve this your child will begin to see you differently— but more importantly, you will begin to think differently about yourself. You will become a person in your own right, with your own interests and convictions. You will be separate from your bullying child, and not subject to his domineering style. He should not be at the centre of your world— you should be at the centre of his. He should look to you as a source of strength rather than as someone to be abused.

Not that you need only think of yourself, of course, when you are considering how to deal with him. But if you are to be strong enough for him, you will need your self-respect.

AT SCHOOL
Teachers can diminish the dominance of a bully in a similar way: they can ensure that those in his immediate vicinity are strong enough to withstand any threat he may present.

Group work
Children in school should always be looked upon as members of a group as well as being individuals. Experts once believed that bullying only happened in relation to group dynamics and that it did not emanate from a bullying personality. Although this view has receded in popularity, the importance of group work is still acknowledged.

Bullying can be directly and indirectly countered by dividing a class into small groups of no more than six pupils. The pupils are given tasks to share and must later report their findings or present a piece of work to the whole group. The concept appears banal, since topic work is often undertaken in this way, until it is looked upon as an anti-bullying strategy. By manipulating the composition of the groups the teacher can place bullies with controlling, countervailing personalities, and thereafter work to the point where such controls may not be necessary.

Group work teaches cooperative learning skills; it can deal directly with issues such as bullying if it is employed in the teaching of such subjects as personal and social education. If at the very beginning a teacher is unsure where to place children, she could ask them all to write down in private which other two children they would like to have in their group. Those whom nobody wanted could be placed with appropriate personalities: the bullies with two other strong personalities and the victims with children who would support and help them. Other children would be assorted according to their social relationships. Teachers who have used this technique have found that children become more accepting and supportive of each other, are more helpful, and have fewer racial prejudices.

The fact that you have given the bully duties and responsibilities (p. 91) does not mean that you have satisfied his need for power and dominance, unless you allow him to abuse his position. Remember that one of the reasons (see p. 107) for awarding him privileges was in order that in the event of needing sanctions you could take them away. His need to be dominant may also, of course, be counteracted by giving praise and pleasure to the bully when he is being passive.

HIS HOSTILITY TO THE WORLD AROUND HIM

A child will regard the world around him as hostile if he is threatened by it. He will react with anger

1   when he cannot get his own way;
2   when he feels criticised;
3   when he feels that a situation is unjust or unfair.

You will need to focus on providing a safe and caring environment for him. This essentially means providing firm boundaries and controls; it does not mean that you should sit down and ask him how he feels. We have discussed how rules and schedules can help you to do this, and how you must strengthen yourself if you are to be the detached and controlling power that you need to be (see p. 93). You will need also to learn how to prevent your child having angry outbursts: the longer he can go without letting himself down in this way, the more chance there will be for a positive self-image to be reinforced.

To avoid angry outbursts, you need to look carefully at each of the three reasons for them.

1 When he cannot get his own way

We are all angry when we cannot get our own way. To avoid this we have to look at what we want and to decide whether it is within our reach.

AT HOME

At the beginning of each day, sit with your child and tell him what is going to happen. Plan the day fully and, if he persistently objects to any part of it, consider a compromise. Before the day starts, you must be clear on what you have both agreed. If he is to go out on his own, discuss what he is going to do and where he is going to be: most bullying occurs in the absence of parents who allow their children to roam where they will.

Apart from exerting your control in this way, you will be making sure that your child does not become frustrated. If he says that he is going to meet a friend, ask what he will do if the friend is not in. Make sure that you go into as much detail as possible. You will thus be gaining control over him even when you are not with him, and he will benefit by sensing your concern. If he appears to disregard your interest, ask him all the same. He will eventually see it as part of the routine, and despite what you may think he will feel more secure because of your comments. When he returns, ask where he has been and what he has been doing. Do not be judgemental—you should be encouraging him to speak freely, not to keep quiet.

Later, when you feel that you can begin to talk about your concerns and worries, do so. As the relationship with your child improves it will be possible to increase your demands on him.

Remember that to avoid angry outbursts you must communicate with him; you must tell him of the plans for the day and the week. When change is necessary, discuss it with him as soon as possible. Be firm about essential changes, and he will accept them: the golden rule is to give him as much notice as possible. He needs time to adjust to change.

AT SCHOOL

It is easier in school to project clear plans for the day, since this is the purpose of the timetable. But although it may not be so easy to provide personal objectives that are realistic and attainable, it is essential to do so in the case of any child who may present behavioural difficulties. While others can adapt and can cope with failure, the bully is unable to tolerate anything that threatens him. He needs to have work set that is within his capability. Undoubtedly, he cannot simply be left to get on with it: he will need a great deal of personal reassurance.

Some bullies have difficulty with the basic skills of reading, writing and arithmetic; if the teacher just assumes that these skills are present, behavioural difficulties will escalate.

2 When he feels criticised

The bully could be seen as someone who, underneath his bravado, has poor self-esteem. As mentioned earlier, this is questioned by research that indicates that, unlike the child who is merely aggressive, the bully does not necessarily have a low self-esteem. When he reacts to criticism he does so only because his attention has been focused on a potential victim. He is not necessarily reacting aggressively to whatever that person may have said or done. His reaction to criticism will, however, vary according to his development: as he passes through adolescence into adulthood his self-image changes (Chapter 3) and he may become increasingly sensitive.

AT HOME

You, the parent, will need to focus on yourself again. When you speak to your child:

1 Do not use swear words.
2 Do not deride his appearance.

3   Do not mock his friends.

1   If you use swear words your manner will be both derisory and disrespectful. No matter how your child speaks or acts, he needs you to speak as a respectful adult. When you do not, he will interpret it as derogatory and demeaning. It will be seen as humiliating because you will be reducing yourself to his level, and in doing so mocking him.

2   Remember that he can do little about his physical appearance, and his dress and hairstyle are his own and you will only escalate matters if you criticise them.

3   If you mock his friends you will be criticising him. He may have heavily identified with one of them; they are his heroes and he becomes all that they believe in. When you criticise his friends, pop stars or sporting heroes you are making a direct personal assault.

As he grows into his teens, be aware that his beliefs will go hot and cold; never criticise him for a lack of consistency. Be aware that he is exploring and in the process of choosing whether or not to leave you behind (adolescence, Chapter 3).

When you speak to your child:

1   Make it clear that you are rejecting not him, but his behaviour.
2   Look for the subtext in his conversation.
3   Recognise his feelings and do not insist on logic.

1   Always be clear about the way you want him to behave, and never hesitate to let him know when his behaviour is unacceptable. It is important, though, that you tell him in such a way that he does not feel that he, as a person, is being condemned. Be quite clear that it is his behaviour that you are not willing to accept.

It is not difficult to do this. Whenever you speak to him about a certain aspect of his behaviour, simply state that you are having difficulty in coping with it. Make sure that he understands which behaviour you are talking about. Try to discuss it with him as though he too were outside it, separate from it. Discuss a strategy that you may both employ to overcome the problem.

2 When he is speaking to you, try to understand what he is really saying. Can you sense the feeling underlying his words? If your child is a bully this could be difficult, since he may appear to have no feelings at all. However, you may be able to hear another message on the surface. If, for example, he is becoming very angry and saying that he isn't coming to his auntie's at the weekend because he thinks she's horrible, he may be telling you the opposite, especially if going to auntie's was not on your agenda.

3 When your child is speaking, he will often be fumbling through his feelings. If he is raging around the house and being incoherent, or if you are trying to have a conversation with him and he does not respond to logic, do not attempt to annihilate him. He is not thinking, he is feeling—and he is in no position to be rational, especially when he is under any kind of pressure from you.

Let him settle before you speak, and if there appears to be no reason in his reply, simply accept it. If you are discussing one of your special requirements, make sure that you are firm. Do not shout and become irrational yourself. Remain calm: he is relying on your coolness and logic.

AT SCHOOL

Teachers should never criticise the bully in front of others. It may be tempting to do so as a way of hurting him, and public humiliation will achieve this as surely as anything will. But to use the tactics of the bully on the bully himself can only initiate an increasingly vicious spiral downwards in terms of relationships and behaviour. If the teacher becomes a bully he may enjoy momentary pleasure, but he will increasingly rely on fear for his control.

A bully *should* be confronted, but in private. In this way he can be effectively dealt with, but not destroyed: he will have been left with a way out, an opportunity for restitution. The teacher can make heavy demands on the bully in private, and neither will lose face whether these are or are not fulfilled. The benefit of the technique is that the child remains in school, and has a further opportunity to get things right. As long as the teacher has approached the problem as a question of unacceptable behaviour rather than as a rejection of the child, he will be able to retain a positive relationship with him.

3 When he feels that a situation is unjust or unfair

Whether or not a situation is unfair depends to some extent on the perception of the person making the judgement. You need to be aware that difficult children may have a very different view from yours when it comes to fairness. In general terms they are hypersensitive, and will often see criticism and unfairness where none is intended. Focus on the need to communicate slowly and carefully with your difficult child; remain calm, and be patient when you are explaining matters to him.

AT HOME
Concentrate on explaining everything to your child. Do not keep him in the dark when it comes to family events. Make sure that he has a clear picture in his mind of what is happening around him. You may say that he is too much in your life anyway, and that the less he knows the better; your inclination may be to keep him out of everything. But he will interpret this as confirmation of his belief that he is disliked and unwanted—and, of course, he may be right. If you really wish to help him you must take some giant leaps, and this is one of them!

Involve him more in your affairs, and you may find that he begins to invest in you. If he is more a part of things, then he will not see so much injustice in what you do. He will have been part of the planning, and will be more able to accept change rather than apportioning blame.

AT SCHOOL
Teachers should clearly define requirements, as far as fairness is concerned, in terms of the regulations of the whole school. In their classrooms they should involve pupils in the formulation of procedures and rules, and regular meetings should be held for this purpose. In addition, any student

who feels that something unfair has happened should know that he can see his teacher privately at a set time during the week. This would enable bullying to be regularly monitored and would provide each child with an opportunity to disclose any problems in confidence.

Group work (p. 94) can help enormously when it comes to preventing a sense of unfairness: an individual can more easily present an injustice for consideration as a group proposal for public discussion than he can on his own. Furthermore, pupils can be helped in this way to learn to tolerate the views of others.

The key to avoiding a sense of injustice is good communication. In the case of those children who are likely to misinterpret actions or intent, there is a special need for rules and regulations to be clearly stated, and an even greater need for them to learn how to consider the views of others.

HIS INABILITY TO SENSE THAT BULLYING IS WRONG OR TO EMPATHISE WITH HIS VICTIM

If a child is to realise what is right and what is wrong, it is necessary for him to feel the implications of his actions on those around him. If he interprets everything in terms only of himself he will live for the gratification of his needs. He must see himself in relation to others; if he does not, and if he has a tendency to excessive aggression, he will intimidate to achieve his ends and bully for his pleasure. You will need, therefore, to concentrate on one of two factors:

1   the bully's need for education in 'the feeling states';
2   his need for training in social skills.

Which you prefer will depend on whether you believe that a leopard can really change his spots.

If you feel that the bully will never be able to appreciate what others feel, you will concentrate on providing him with an opportunity to copy or adopt social skills. These will enable him to live peacefully alongside others. He will learn to use them as a physically handicapped person may learn to use crutches. If, on the other hand, you feel that he is capable of feeling and that he can be made more sensitive, you will provide opportunities for him to develop an appreciation of the 'feeling states'.

If you are sensible, you will adopt both approaches.

AT HOME:

1   Whenever you talk to your partner, try to emphasise how you feel about things. Do not simply state facts and figures; let him know how you feel about what has happened during the day, and so on. Share your feelings in a calm and controlled way. Encourage your partner to do the same. In this way you will be providing a good model for the bully.

Make sure, however, that you do not give full vent to your negative feelings about the bully. Resist doing this in any way other than a controlled and caring one, and when you have to sanction him make sure that you do it in private. Simply allow him to exist in a climate where people show their feelings, when times are good, by expressing them, but restrict themselves to an objective approach when it comes to anything else.

You may in this way be able to induce in him a consideration for the feelings of others.

When you are watching TV with him, comment on the way actors may be feeling, or on how you would feel if you were in their position. You may after a while feel able to ask him how he feels about other people, places or issues. If you have shared activities with him (Chapter 5), refer back to them and mention your good feelings about them; express your excitement at the thought of future trips with him. When you receive presents, express your delight; when you receive bad news, say how sad it makes you feel.

You may be faced with a blanket response to all of this. It is invariably a long process, and you may need to persist over many months before you see the slightest response.

A more direct approach which would rely less on yourself would be to encourage your child to develop an interest. Sport, in particular, can break a negative attitude to life; it can provide a sense of purpose and achievement and lead to consideration of others. Working as a member of a team can also provide a sense of belonging, and be the first step away from selfishness.

Research possibilities at your local library. If you discover something that might interest him, contact the organisation concerned and persuade one of its members to approach your son on the basis that they have heard from his school that he might be interested. Not all sports are team activities, but they all provide an opportunity to relate to others through a common interest, and can thus lead to the development of an appreciation and consideration for the needs of others.

2   Providing your child with social skills can be achieved by good communication. But in purely practical terms it is all about telling him what to say and when to say it; it is about showing him what to do, and when you want him to do it.

Here we want to focus on helping him to appreciate what is right and what is wrong. But in teaching him the right and wrong way to behave do not emphasise the rights and wrongs of every situation and issue: you do not want him to be over-critical towards everyone. This is what you do next:

a   Make a priority list of those times of the day when your child's behaviour could be improved.
b   Select the least important behaviour.
c   Modify it.

Use this method:

Explain
Choose a time when your child is settled and alone with you, and explain precisely how he should carry out whatever behaviour you have chosen. Resist being judgemental about his past performance. Behave as if he has not been told this before, even though you may have told him many times. You need to assure him that, despite his behaviour, you are not rejecting him. Treat the matter as similar to teaching etiquette: he needs to know precisely what to do and what to say.

Demonstrate
Demonstrate the skill to the child in private. Refer to episodes on film or TV where his heroes showed how they could do this.

Rehearse
Rehearse the skill with him in private. Avoid telling him what not to do—concentrate on what he *should* do. As you rehearse, clearly and precisely explain the sequence of actions and words.

Implement
Tell him when you will be expecting him to utilise this skill. For example, rather than showing him what to do and then leaving him with a vague directive, limit the new behaviour to a specific mealtime such as breakfast. You must decide whether to be present or not. This will depend on the relationship you have with the child: he may react negatively if you are there—if so, ask another adult to tell you how he behaved. He may, of course, need you to be there to show off his new behaviour; if so, make sure that you reinforce it with a quiet smile of approval.

Do not over-react: you are teaching him social skills, not a mechanism whereby he can control you.

Review
Focus on the new skill for no more than a week, and then have a rest. During this time, when you have eased off, the child may suddenly decide to implement what he has been taught. After the rest period, move up the list to the next item. Begin to teach this in the same way as the first. If this process is repeated, you will eventually come to the end of your list. When you do, cycle through it again, gradually performing a number of skills at the same time.

Do not become disheartened if your teaching seems to be having no effect, and remember that children absorb far more than you may imagine. They will often surprise by criticising you for behaviour that is against your teaching and that you imagined they had completely forgotten, or refer to what you have said when they are trying to win an argument. They will learn from you what is right and wrong if you are consistent and if you have the stamina to keep repeating it. Whether they actually behave in a way that is consistent with this will depend on their general level of stability and the environment in which they find themselves.

AT SCHOOL

The most important part of a school anti-bullying policy should be the statement that bullying is wrong and that it will not be tolerated. It has to be overtly asserted and reinforced in the approach that every member of the school adopts (Chapter 10). It must pervade the curriculum and be embodied as a clear principle in the life of the school.

The bully should feel the full weight of the school pressing in on him with regard to the question of whether his actions are right or wrong. At class level there should be an emphasis on group work. Here the teacher may manipulate and control him, bringing up ethical and moral issues for discussion in anonymity (p. 95).

The bully should be given the opportunity to attend specialist counselling sessions, where his apparent lack of conscience may be addressed in detail; special programmes should be implemented to help him recognise his feelings, as well as the feelings and behaviour of others. He may, for example, be led to acknowledge signals that people use to denote thoughts and feelings. Many children find it difficult to distinguish between various facial expressions; others may be unable to understand that when a person is wringing her hands and pacing up and down, for example, she is agitated and in distress.

This specialist facility should be available in all schools and for all children: those clearly at risk—and there will always be a considerable number—could thereby receive extra support with personal problems. Bullying is only one of the many behavioural difficulties that children present; along with other unwanted behaviour, it is often the result of an inadequate focus on the development and psychology of children within our schools.

HIS INABILITY TO TAKE RESPONSIBILITY FOR HIS ACTIONS

The bully will not accept responsibility for his bullying. He will say that his victim deserves it, or, perhaps, that he 'wound me up'. Look carefully at this phrase, since it embodies all that is wrong with the attitude that some children have to their behaviour. It clearly indicates that they think they can be controlled by others and that they have no responsibility for their own actions; if nothing else, it is a mere excuse and should be recognised as such.

You will need to focus on making the bully aware that he must own his actions.

AT HOME

Being responsible

Whenever you and your partner speak, get into the habit (if you aren't already) of using the personal pronoun 'I' and not 'You'. For example, instead of saying, 'You feel terrible when you have to get up early', say 'I feel terrible when I have to get up early.' This may seem an insignificant exercise, but if you check your speech you will be surprised at how often you appear to disown things in this way.

When things go wrong and you are disappointed, try to resist blaming anyone. You may find this very difficult, but it is worthwhile. You can make it easier by thinking to yourself, 'Can I be the one to think of a solution to this problem?' People tend to blame others when they do not know what to do. Be the person who takes the positive approach: look upon your problems as an opportunity to show your initiative. Above all, do not go down with your difficulties; remain separate and in control (Chapter 8).

If you do adopt this attitude to life, it will be absorbed by your child. By accepting responsibility for your life you will be teaching him to do the same.

Making him responsible

If your child has specific responsibilities such as taking the dog for a walk and making sure that he is fed, he will find it difficult to avoid accepting the responsibilities that ensue. Make sure that he has a number of such duties—it will generally encourage him to feel responsible. (Incidentally, children will often accept responsibility for animals and relate better to them than they would to another person.)

In addition, allow him to accept responsibility for his mistakes by talking to him in private about any unacceptable behaviour, setting it in the context of the need for him to accept responsibility for his actions in general. Do not persist in presenting him with any indisputable evidence, or in destroying him with your superior logic. Remain calm, and be aware that he needs a way out. If he appears not to listen, simply state your requirements and the need for *all of us* to take responsibility for our actions. On a later occasion, when you are not there, he may do what you have suggested.

AT SCHOOL

We have already mentioned the viability of giving the bully duties and responsibilities. As well as being useful as sanctions when they are withdrawn, they carry the added bonus, if he fully assumes them—which he well may—of teaching him what the word 'responsibility' means.

In small group settings he should be given exercises that contain an element of choice; whatever he decides should result in a consequence for himself and for others. In this way he may learn that he has control over his destiny, and will thereby gain an increased sense of responsibility.

Outdoor pursuits and physical disciplines can provide the bully with an opportunity to shine; with his likely extra strength and physical prowess, he may assume a position of leadership and responsibility. When he physically experiences the consequences of his actions, as in sport, the need to be responsible may register, especially when he is placed in situations—such as in a team—where he relies on others as much as they rely on him. Physical discipline in itself can promote a feeling of self-worth and personal control (see Chapter 8).

Teachers should avoid regarding the bully as somebody else's responsibility. If they look upon him as a challenge, using their training and imagination they may find his improved behaviour and sense of responsibility very rewarding. However much they are inclined, they should stop blaming him and his parents for his behaviour. To do so is to adopt his style and to disclaim responsibility; it is to provide a role model at the mercy of his surroundings, one who refuses to take a positive, pro-active approach to life.

CONCLUSION

The needs of the bully as described above are those he has in addition to the needs he would have as a normal child. Because of his temperament, these normal needs are also exaggerated and require special attention (Chapter 5). The scenario for anyone hoping to deal with the bully is therefore complex, and requires specialist attention if the root cause of his behaviour is to be addressed. To complement any such facilities, if they exist, parents and schools must do all they can to provide a controlling and caring environment.

Responding to the needs of the bully requires imagination and a great deal of perseverance. I hope that this rather long chapter has given you food for thought, and that you have been able to select some ideas from it that are meaningful to you.

7 Managing the Victim

When people think about bullying, a necessary part of their scenario is often a weak, pathetic victim. They apportion blame to him as much as they do to the bully. But this attitude breeds complacency when it comes to dealing with the bully, and neglect when it comes to caring for the victim. It is based on the assumption that those who have an aggressive personality have a right to inherit the world. Little credit is given to the contribution made by less aggressive but more thoughtful personalities to the breadth and quality of our existence.

While it is necessary to examine the needs of bullies if you are to effectively deal with them (Chapter 6), it is essential when dealing with incidents of bullying that you are seen to act (Chapter 8). Parents of children who are victimised should take a strong stand when it comes to facing up to the bully: they should do all they can to see that his behaviour is not ignored. Turning a blind eye to bullying is to condone it and sends to the victim the message that he is at fault.

Victims do have special needs, and it is to these that we are now going to give our attention. But in doing so our aim is to defeat the purpose of the bully; in no way are we condemning the victim.

THE PASSIVE VICTIM

His need to feel less anxious and more secure

A child who has a high level of anxiety may have been emotionally fragile from birth (Chapter 4). He will be more sensitive to the world around him than other children, and his anxiety will have been intensified by his inability to cope with the circumstances of his life. You will need to focus on providing a secure environment for him.

AT HOME

A safe environment is one which accepts a child for what he is; it is one that does not make heavy demands on him, and where people make a special effort to recognise him for his good points. They notice him and talk to him; they make favourable comments; they offer a great deal of praise and encouragement.

In his immediate environment there is order and there are routines. Meals are at set times, and certain events occur regularly on the same day. There is a level of expectation regarding behaviour, but it is within the child's reach and he feels good when he achieves it. Above all, there are people who are significant to him. These people stand for something in his mind; they are his role models, and he needs them because they provide him with a sense of purpose.

If you are to make your anxious child feel less so, there may be specific things to do relating to his fear of being bullied, and these we shall be dealing with in Chapter 8. Meanwhile, we shall focus on you again, as well as your child.

EXERCISE SEVEN

A   Your personality:

1   List three things that you hate about yourself.
2   List three things that you like about yourself.

When you have done this, repeat it for your child:

B   Your child's personality:

1   List three things that you dislike about him.
2   List three things that you like about him.

You may think that these are just short lists, but be prepared for them to take a long time to complete! And they may provide you with food for thought:

A1   If you hate yourself there could be a need to reassess your ideal model—the image of what you think you should be (Chapter 4). Most people's personal frustrations are caused by their having an unrealistic idea of what they should aspire to. Look at the list you have just made and decide whether in reality you can change any of the things on it. If you can, then make a determined effort to do so—don't just talk about it. If you cannot, then accept yourself for what you are and decide how you can best cope with your personality. You might turn your defects to your advantage.

A2 Concentrate on these, and you will be getting things right. You need to believe in yourself, to recognise your own strengths. Focus on these, and not on your weaknesses. Do not always compare yourself with others. Each of us has his own strengths and contributes in his own way.

B1 When you consider those things that you dislike about your child, check back to see whether they are the same as those you dislike about yourself. This is often the case. If the two lists do not coincide, ask yourself whether the items you have listed here are, in fact, those qualities that you fear you may have within you.

We often project our own personalities on to our child, and this can only lead to problems. It is natural to feel for your child, but do make every effort to see him as a separate human being with his own capabilities, hopes and aspirations.

B2 You must focus on the things you like about your child and encourage his strengths. The idea that parents (and schools) should always concentrate on a child's weakness is wrong; a high level of self-esteem is necessary before any weakness can be remedied, and this is best achieved by cultivating strengths.

If you are to help your child become less anxious you will need to feel more secure about yourself. To feel safe, he needs to have people around him who are strong—not powerful and domineering, but sure of themselves. They should like themselves and have enough confidence to fill him with a sense of security (Chapter 4).

AT SCHOOL

Schools need to install an effective infrastructure if fewer vulnerable children are to be left at the mercy of the bully (Chapter 10). Clear rules and regulations and a timetable that has a recognisable structure can go a long way towards providing a safe environment for every child. A clear anti-bullying policy is essential for those who are more vulnerable.

There are a number of specific strategies that can be employed by individual teachers to diminish the general level of anxiety among these children:

Tutors

Children who are known to be vulnerable should be allotted a special person in the school to whom they can turn whenever they need support. This special tutor should have regular meetings with the child.

The child would not always use the sessions to report bullying: they would be regarded as preventive in that, if he were assured about things in general, he would feel more confident and able to withstand pressure. Children joining a new school, for instance, worry about timetables and homework and are unsure of the requirements. The more anxious child will be desperate to please and fearful of failure.

Teachers should ask about possible difficulties before children arrive in their class, and make tutorial time available. To avoid stigma attaching to the target pupils, they should make this time available for one or two more resilient ones as well.

Class teachers may make the most appropriate tutors, but each school needs to decide on its own particular policy (Chapter 10). A useful arrangement is to allow a tutor to stay with a child as he moves through the school, thus providing further stability. The ideal is for every child to have a tutor for these purposes, but the effectiveness of such an arrangement has to be balanced against the heavy demands that the more vulnerable child might place on the system. Bullies, of course, should have the same priority as victims.

Small groups
Small subgroups will not only facilitate cooperative learning techniques, they will also offer a setting in which the anxious child may gain confidence (Chapter 6).

Paired duties and responsibilities
The anxious child should be paired with a more secure child, and together they should be given duties and responsibilities. After a while the anxious child should be encouraged to perform these on his own. Pairing him with another may not only provide him with an opportunity to gain confidence, but will possibly lead to a permanent friendship.

Positioning
Anxious children should be placed in the vicinity of the teacher, and in a position where little or, preferably, no eye contact can be made with the bully.

Non-verbal work
The value of non-verbal work with the more anxious child cannot be overemphasised. Such children are often afraid or unable to express their fears and aspirations verbally. In art, drama, music and play their feelings may be made clear to all who see the potential that these subjects have for revealing problems.

However, the most effective way in which a teacher may provide a safe and secure environment for the more anxious child is to deal firmly with the bully. Not only does she have to state that bullying will not be allowed, she has to back her words with action (Chapter 8).

His need to be less cautious, less quiet and sensitive
A child is cautious when he fears for his safety. When you provide him with a safe and secure setting (p. 109), he will be more confident and able to take risks. When he is unable to take risks, it is because he fears failure: if he is provided with an accepting environment rather than an excessively exacting one, he will feel more able to make mistakes.
    If a child is quiet and sensitive, it is because he does not

want to be in the limelight. Because he has little confidence in himself he prefers to be in the shadows.

Focus on his need to develop self-confidence.

AT HOME

The warm environment that you have created will go a long way towards helping your child to become more confident. And you can develop his self-confidence even more by taking him out of your home and encouraging him to mix with other people. If you can arrange this, he will begin to assume an identity separate from yours; his sense of personal worth will increase.

A good way to approach things is to begin by thinking of his particular interests. (Be sure that you do not foist any of your own hidden aspirations on to him (p. 118).) Then, think of another child who may be interested in the same activity, and contact his parents. Perhaps you could make shared transport arrangements with them, and in this way both you and your child might begin to develop a network of friends.

As already mentioned, physical activities are both physiologically and psychologically beneficial. Indeed, many would say that they are essential for a feeling of self-worth. Every effort, therefore, should be made to involve your child. Remember that it is not simply the physical exercise that can strengthen a person: it is its inherent self-discipline that results in a feeling of wholeness. If possible, get him interested in one of the martial arts that directly promote self-respect through disciplined exercise. Such skills can also promote a more assertive but controlled aggressive approach.

Your child may, of course, have completely different interests; but being a member of the local branch of model railway enthusiasts rather than the karate club will still give him a sense of belonging.

He needs to feel separate from you, so do try to promote his own interests rather than make him an extension of yourself.

If you feel that he is too quiet and sensitive, it will usually be because of his lack of confidence. It could be, however, that he is being so just to please you. Perhaps you subconsciously demand quietness and sensitivity. Perhaps you need them.

AT SCHOOL

In school a vulnerable child will be given confidence by the strength and ethos of the protecting environment around him. He will also develop confidence by receiving a great deal of personal help, praise and encouragement.

When attempting to develop confidence in the more vulnerable child, the teacher should in a variety of subject areas:

1 pair the pupil with a more confident classmate;
2 make a list of three assets that the pupil displays;
3 provide graded opportunities for these assets to be publicly displayed by the pair, and later by the pupil alone.

For example, a child who is good at drawing might make an illustration to accompany a short talk given by his classmate, say, in school assembly; later, the cautious child might feel able to repeat the talk to his class. And there are other such simple exercises that can promote his self-confidence and reduce his need for caution.

It is essential to lead the child gradually into a position where he is not afraid to make mistakes, where he is strong enough to accept failure.

It would be inappropriate to force him to take part in a school production or to play rugby. You may encourage him to do so, but be sensitive to the possibility of worsening his condition. Aggressive physical activities can leave scars for life. Although, as already mentioned, sport *can* be the perfect way to help a child to grow in confidence, teachers should be aware of pupils' sensitivity when it comes to physical prowess (Chapter 3). They should never assume that all pupils will benefit from a particular sport, and should offer a variety of pursuits. Moreover, they need to be aware that vulnerable children will not be toughened up by being press-ganged into an aggressive team game.

The emotionally fragile child may look like a rugby player but be trembling in his boots at the prospect of his clumsiness being revealed. The good PE teacher will be sensitive to the needs of the vulnerable child, and will not bully him into participation.

His need to improve his self-esteem

The victim has a low self-esteem. Some believe that he was born with it, others that his life circumstances have cowed him into believing that he has no value. A child with low self-esteem feels that he is worthless when compared with those around him.

Your child should appreciate the assets of others and be happy for them. And you should focus on his becoming more aware of his own.

AT HOME

The caring home will induce a sense of self-worth in a child: he will feel that family members value him for what he is and not for what they expect him to be. If your child is vulnerable, you will need to make a special effort to project your acceptance and respect.

When you speak to him:

1 Avoid being critical of him.
2 Praise him whenever you can.
3 Take every opportunity to project the positive aspects of his personality. Slip reminders of how you think of him into your conversation.

When you speak of others:

1 Do not always criticise and complain about them.
2 Praise them and extol their good qualities.
3 Ask him to tell you what he likes about them.

Allow him to express himself freely. Do not be threatened by any opposing views that he may present—on the contrary, be encouraged by them. Show by your example that it is possible to admire other people without feeling bad about yourself. To put it another way, help him to realise that to feel good about himself he does not have to feel bad about others.

In your conversations with him try to project the message

that we are all different, that each person has unique qualities, and that each has a part to play. Talk to him about any
hero that he may have; gently bring him to the realisation
that his hero has some faults—but that he is a hero all the
same, with good points and bad points like the rest of us.

AT SCHOOL

As we have seen, a child's self-esteem may be promoted by
a gradual introduction to duties and responsibilities. It may
be slowly enhanced through small-group activities and by
the development of personal relationships through paired
project work.

All vulnerable children need an extra dose of praise and
encouragement, though few relish the thought of being publicly acclaimed. But if a child is able to produce tangible
evidence of his efforts he can be in the spotlight without
suffering personal embarrassment. Paintings and drawings
can be displayed, as can his written work. Practical subjects
such as technology can result in three-dimensional pieces of
work that give such children an enormous, if private, feeling
of status when they are on public view.

Having his work displayed has a special significance for
the more vulnerable child.

To counteract the vulnerable child's tendency to feel
worthless in relation to others, teachers should:

1 emphasise the fact that each child is in school to improve
   himself and to help others to do the same;
2 denigrate the notion of one child beating another.

This is particularly important in PE and games, where there
is a tendency to promote an attitude of annihilation. The
purpose of both individual and team games should be for
the improvement of the individual or the team. It should
not be to beat the opposition.

It is a fine point to make, but extremely pertinent when
we are considering the plight of the victim. Denigrating the
opposition in order to make himself feel good is a characteristic that he shares with the bully. Entrenched in this mode
of interaction, they become frustrated instead of elated when
faced with a superior performance; the bully reacts by being

impulsively aggressive, and the victim withdraws into self-pity and despair. Schools should do all they can to reverse this tendency.

His need to develop more friendships

Friendships usually arise from common interests. Should a child have no interests, it is unlikely that he will develop friendships. Interests define personalities as much as do occupations. It is important for your vulnerable child to have interests in order that he can become a member of a group.

AT HOME
Focus on providing him with possible interests or, if he already has some, encourage these. Take the initiative when it comes to his joining a club or society. But never presume that you can establish friendships for him by simply inviting other children into the home. The vulnerable child will usually resist any such move—he sees his home as his territory, his safe haven.

A   If your passive child is not interested in anything:

1   Look at your own interests.
2   Make sure you have a definite enthusiasm that would be appropriate for him too.
3   Insist that he join you, albeit reluctantly.

When you are being firm about him coming with you, he may, as he resists, suggest that he wants to do something else instead. Fine. For if he does your technique has worked, since your intention is for him to have an interest of some sort or other. At this stage, be firm about what it is that he is going to do. Make sure that his interest is regularly pursued, and then follow B below.

But if he goes along with you and adopts *your* interest, you can point him in the direction of enthusiasts of his own age. In this way you will be able gradually to introduce him to new friends.

B   If your child has some interests:

1   Accept them, no matter how insignificant you think they are.

2 Show an interest by asking him questions about his hobby.

3 If there is a magazine related to it, point him towards it when you are next in the newsagent's.

4 Find out the contacts for this particular interest at your local library. There are societies for everything!

5 Speak to the contact person and explain the situation in general terms. Arrange to take your child to one of their meetings. Make sure that he has a person to link up with.

If, after all your efforts, you are concerned about your child's lack of friends, temper your anxiety with the notion that not everyone is as gregarious as the next person. As with all our personality traits, we are on a curve: at one end of the spectrum are the super-gregarious, and at the other are those who prefer to be on their own. Most of us like to have time with others *and* time on our own. Look carefully at your requirements in this respect, and make sure that you are not imposing your ideal model (p. 56) on to your child.

AT SCHOOL
Friendships, or the lack of them, are obvious in the classroom: isolated children are easily noticed.

Small groups
Teachers should see the arrangement of children into subgroups as a priority. In academic and practical work those children who have few friends can be helped enormously by being placed in appropriate groups.

Free time
Free time poses many problems for the passive child, and special consideration should be given to the victim (as well as to the bully) when free time (breaktimes and lunchtimes) is being organised (Chapter 10). In essence, their free time should be either closely organised or monitored.

Pen-pals
The shy, passive child can establish friendships through letter-writing. If the remainder of the class do the same, he will have something further in common with them and something different to report.

Hobbies
Teachers should know the details of each child's personal life if they are to relate to him. Wanting to know such minutiae shows concern and facilitates control of the situation. If they know of the passive child's interests they can link him up with someone else in the school who has similar interests. There may even be the possibility of a club being formed around him.

Mentors
When a vulnerable child attends a new school or class, another child should be appointed to look after him. This child should accept responsibility for the victim, offering him support and encouragement. After a week, the responsibility can be passed to another child. If the mentor system lasts a full term, the passive child will have been introduced to a number of children and may have found one particular friend.

His need to be more aggressive
Every child has a certain amount of aggression in him, and some have more than others, as we have noted. A child's aggression can be increased by his being rewarded for being so. If his aggression reaps no reward, he will tend to be passive. And being passive means that you feel that you have no control over your life; you must wait for the world around you to change things. You feel there is nothing you can do to effect change.

Focus on providing experiences that will indicate to your child that he *can* change the things around him.

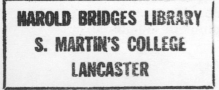
HAROLD BRIDGES LIBRARY
S. MARTIN'S COLLEGE
LANCASTER

AT HOME

His environment
1 Discuss with your child the idea of changing the furniture around in the lounge. Listen to his views. If the lounge has to stay as it is, suggest that he do it to his own room.
2 Discuss the idea of redesigning the garden. Again, if he has suggestions, consider whether they are viable. If they are not, provide him with a part of the garden that he *can* change.
3 Ask him to trim the hedge or cut the lawn. Tell him they need to be neat and tidy.
4 Propose to him that he should wash the car. If he does a good job, reward him. Insist that you want it to look like a new car, so much so that the neighbours will not recognise it.
5 Ask him to clean the windows. Impress on him that they must be done to perfection, transformed and crystal-clear.

All this practical work should be rewarded with a previously agreed amount of money, and your child should be allowed to spend it on anything that does not seriously threaten his or your welfare. Unless he has financial resources, he will find it difficult to object.

His self-image
1 Look through clothing catalogues. Discuss how people dress. Ask him how he would like to appear. Allow him to dress up, then congratulate him on his imagination. Comment on how he has been able to transform himself.
2 Comment on hairstyles; ask your child how he would like his hair. Take him to the barber's and encourage him to have a different cut.
3 When you are buying clothes, as long as it is within your budget encourage him to make a choice. If the chosen item turns out to be not quite right, encourage him to return it and to make another choice.
4 Buy him some cheap aftershave (or, if your child is a girl, some perfume), and ask him what he thinks of it. If he refuses to use it, be encouraged by his self-assertion.

5   Whenever possible, provide a variety of food. In this way you are giving him another opportunity for choice. And comment on his choice, making him feel that it has made an impression on you.

If possible, provide your child with an allowance so that he can be encouraged to pay for his own clothes and so on— far better if he can work for some of his money, too.

Relationships

1   Try to place your child in such a position that it is he who determines what you will be doing on a particular day. Make this day his. Be consistent, and follow through with his suggestions unless they would seriously jeopardise your safety or your bank balance!
2   Allow him to make the final decision on where you will go for your holidays—again, as long as it is financially possible for you.
3   On certain evenings allow him the freedom to choose TV programmes.
4   On Friday nights allow him to stay up as long as he wants to.
5   On Saturday mornings allow him to get up when he wants to.

Activities

The passive child may benefit by being introduced to clubs and societies (p. 118), particularly sporting ones. By participating in activities that require self-discipline and control, he will become more in charge of himself and more proactive or aggressive with the world around him.

AT SCHOOL
The temptation to simply place the passive child in situations that demand aggression should be resisted. Throwing him in at the deep end will promote his poor self-esteem. Vulnerable children should be introduced gradually to those activities that may be thought to expose them to risk.

Apart from the initiatives already mentioned in this chapter, specialist help may furnish the passive child with skills that will promote assertiveness. Classroom teachers should make themselves aware of these techniques in order that they may adapt them for use with all children, and particularly with those who are vulnerable. They can also assist by teaching social skills to all children and by providing a systematic programme of training in communication and negotiation skills.

As in the home, the child should be given every opportunity to make choices. Rather than taking a diffuse approach to this, the teacher should allocate certain times when activities and exercises involving choice are offered. This does not mean that the child has a choice to do either something or nothing: it means that he must select an activity or a solution to an exercise, and then carry it through to its conclusion.

Care should therefore be taken to devise activities and exercises that can result in the positive reinforcement of choice. If the child is unable to succeed with any of his choices, he will remain passive. If he can change something and experience success, then he will gain a sense of control over his world: he will adopt a more aggressive approach to living.

THE PROVOCATIVE VICTIM

His need to be more focused, more mature and less irritating
Every child is able to focus, and some are able to focus much more than others. Those who find it difficult may do so because of an underlying anxiety. When a child is unable to focus, he is unable to retain information, and this means that he will not be able to acquire the building blocks necessary for learning. If he is unable to learn he will act in an immature way, and in frustration he will irritate and create tension.

Concentrate on providing a safe and secure environment: the provocative victim has the same needs as the passive victim, except that his are greater.

AT HOME
You can provide opportunities for focused thought, but do not force your child into a frenzy of intellectual pursuits: you may only intensify his passivity.

1   Turn the television off, and allow it on only at certain times. Viewing is passive and allows your child's mind to float if he stays in front of the television for too long.
2   Provide materials for alternative activities, but do not tell him to use them.
3   When he is ready he will start to use the Scrabble, the jigsaws, the military games board or whatever else you have supplied.
4   Provide a computer and a mixture of games, but firmly restrict their use to two nights each week.
5   In all these activities join in when you can, but don't intrude when you are not wanted. You will be aware when you are not welcome, and you must respect the wish that your child may have for privacy.

You may discover that he *can* focus: it is simply a matter of his being motivated. Computer games usually do this. You can use them as a tool in their own right, or as an incentive to complete other games. Always look for new incentives: one way of doing this would be to examine the list you made of his assets (p. 110), and then devise incentives based on them.

AT SCHOOL
A child's inability to focus will be alleviated considerably by the creation of an environment in which he feels safe and secure (p. 112). Teachers should be aware of the learning difficulties of the more anxious, vulnerable child (as noted earlier, some have not learned the most basic skills of numeracy and literacy). So they must be supplied with work that they can do, and from which they may progress to a higher level. Programmes for all children should, of course, be differentiated according to individual skills; if they are not, they will become bored and restless.

The short concentration span of the provocative victim can be catered for by offering him alternative activities and exercises. It should never be assumed that every child is capable of sitting in his seat for thirty minutes and performing the same task, and classrooms should be equipped for a multitude of activities. When a child has spent five minutes on a piece of work he may be allowed to put headphones on and enjoy some music, or play on the computer. A week later he may have extended this work period to ten minutes.

All children should be able to enjoy such classroom conditions, but for the child who has a limited concentration span they are essential requirements. Should the special needs of the provocative victim be ignored, he will become less focused: he will act in an immature way that irritates others and creates tension in the classroom.

The provocative victim may, like the bully or the passive victim, benefit by receiving help from specialists who can introduce him to ways of relaxing and focusing. The classroom teacher may implement some of these techniques each day, not just for the provocative victim but for the whole group. As with so many of the strategies aimed at helping the problem child, all children would benefit by learning relaxation techniques, especially if they were persuaded to perform them daily at home.

CONCLUSION

Although we may disregard the victim, he does have our natural sympathy: perhaps we tend to ignore his plight because we cannot bear to feel the pain that he feels or his hate for the bully. Parents, in particular, can easily become embroiled in the emotions of their children, especially those who have a more vulnerable child.

A dilemma is created by the fact that children reflect the anxieties of their parents: so the parent anxious about her child is going to make matters worse. The solution is for parents to try to detach themselves a little from their child—to look at him more objectively, decide what his needs are and try to meet them. They must be both strong in themselves and sensitive to his needs, if they are to help. In this chapter we have looked at the special needs of victims and how parents and teachers may cope with them.

I would urge parents never to accept the advice of anyone regarding their child without careful consideration of all the issues involved. I hope that in this chapter I have introduced you to one or two useful notions.

8 Dealing with Bullying in the Classroom

We have discussed how bullies and victims may be managed. Now it is time to see what may be done when we have to deal with an episode of bullying, and here I address the class teacher specifically.

Although any programme related to human behaviour must be regarded as a long-term project, the very nature of bullying means that something must also be done about it immediately. As already stressed, if it appears that no action is being taken then both the victim and the bully will assume that it is condoned.

Any action that we take must achieve two objectives: it must firmly establish that bullying is unacceptable, and it must try to change the behaviour of the bully and of the victim. Before you take action to combat specific instances of bullying, it is worth considering some tactics that can be employed with the whole group.

THE WHOLE-GROUP APPROACH

1 The big circus act
It is worth remembering the effectiveness of a public display of abhorrence and disgust. The big circus act should be performed only on rare occasions, and with impact, to firmly establish with the group as a whole the basic principle that bullying will never be tolerated. It is called the big circus act because it requires you to perform to the very best of your ability, with all your power and with panache. You are there to protect the innocent, and you display your determination to do so.

The technique is particularly useful when you are not

aware of any specific episodes of bullying but have an uneasy feeling that something is going on. The aim should be to impress the group with the seriousness of your suspicions, and to let the bully know that you are on the verge of tackling the matter directly. It should be to warn him and those on the periphery to stop before it is too late, and to assert to others that they have a duty to report any bullying, that there is the opportunity to speak to you privately, and that whatever they tell you will be kept in absolute confidence.

In short, the technique employs the maxim, 'If the cap fits, wear it.'

Do not doubt the ethics involved here. You are not bullying—you are protecting potential victims. You are also preventing the bully from letting himself down again. The strategy will work only if you are extremely committed to it—so much so that you can assume your position of ringmaster and are prepared to crack your whip whenever necessary. Do not try it if you lack confidence.

2   Peer pressure

Children will always respond to their peers better than to adults, if they have the choice. You can use this to good effect.

If you have organised your group programme interestingly you will have arranged for a variety of trips and treats throughout the term. It is important to do this to create a group feeling—just as important, in fact, as creating incentives such as duties and responsibilities within the classroom. And if you have worked at it there will be many attractive activities and facilities within the classroom.

One of the advantages of your hard work will be that, in the event of your having suspicions that bullying is taking place, these incentives can be withdrawn. You can refer to 'certain people' (no names) who are letting the side down; you can say that you are disappointed, and not willing to spend time organising special events if they are not appreciated. Say that you are not prepared to put in a lot of effort if some people think that their job is to make the lives of others unpleasant. As a group, everyone should be working together to make it a particularly happy time.

To make the technique even more effective, say nothing until the day of the trip and then announce its cancellation. Declare that you are not happy with the behaviour of 'certain people', and that unless there is a dramatic change in attitude the trip scheduled for next week will also be cancelled. You can develop this into a short lecture on the need to care for others and so forth. No discussion is allowed, and the group then gets down to some work.

This may seem to be very harsh on the innocent, but provided the following conditions are fulfilled you will need to do it only once:

1   The incentive must be of great appeal to the majority.
2   You will have already cultivated a sense of group loyalty.
3   The majority of the group respects and likes you.

If you consider using this technique it would be wise to discuss the possibility of it occurring, in general terms, with the parents at the beginning of your relationship with them. Do not be confused about the ethics of punishing all the children for the behaviour of one or two: in doing so you are protecting the interests of every one of them. If you have worked hard for your group they will respect your integrity.

Both the big circus act and the peer-pressure technique must be used very rarely if they are to have effect on the bully. Although you will not have dealt directly with his behaviour, the group will be much more knowledgeable about it than you can imagine. They will demand that he change his ways; and under the illusion that you will not notice, he will most likely comply.

But do not hesitate to investigate bullying fully when you have *more* than the slightest suspicion or sense of unease. You must be aware of the tendency we have to ignore it and to interpret it as normal aggression. It is vital that here you do not simply use the above techniques in the hope that you will have frightened the bully off.

Continually monitor the behaviour of the children in your group, and never fail to grasp the nettle when necessary. To differentiate between normal aggression and bullying is one of your primary responsibilities.

THE INDIVIDUAL APPROACH

Stage One: Investigating

A characteristic of much bullying is that it takes place in secret. Bullies will only bully when there is no apparent risk of their being discovered, so it occurs in places where there is little adult supervision. Victims are invariably fearful of reprisals, should they report the aggressors, and if they pluck up the courage to do so the bullies will profess to the utmost their innocence. So there is always a need to undertake a thorough investigation.

It is often tempting simply to declare that the bully is guilty and that her actions will not be tolerated. But this is not good enough. Whoever is investigating the matter must realise that the thoroughness of his or her investigation will make its mark with all those concerned: it's not what you do—it's the way that you do it! It is always necessary to make it clear to those on the periphery as well as to those involved that you are not at all happy, and that something is being done about it.

Here are some guiding principles relating to the investigative phase of the operation:

1　*Confidentiality*

Never question a child about personal matters in front of others. In the case of a bully, you will invariably stimulate an aggressive outburst as she defends herself. The usual reaction from an older pupil will be for her to storm out in deep-seated resentment or to assault you, either verbally or physically.

A victim will feel acute embarrassment and become extremely apprehensive should you publicly discuss an episode of bullying in which she has been involved. Needless to say, if the bully is publicly confronted at the same time as the victim you will double the embarrassment of both parties.

But you may say that this is fine so long as it stops the bullying, and that the short-lived pain suffered by the participants is of little consequence. I would say that by publicly embarrassing them you will have achieved three things: you will have alienated the bully from the victim even more, and vice versa; you will have alienated both the bully and the victim from yourself; and you will have made sure that if any more bullying takes place in your group, nobody is ever going to let you know.

So when investigating an episode of bullying, do all you can to retain privacy and confidentiality. You will find that, if you do, it will be easier to come to a fair and just conclusion. Pupils will tell you things in private that they never would if they had to speak in front of others, and you will gain a more accurate impression of the consensus of opinion. By approaching the matter in this way you will be able to deal with the bully very firmly and with the victim very sympathetically; and you will be able to preserve the self-esteem of both, while remaining supportive and constructive.

Privacy and confidentiality should be primary characteristics of any whole-school policy employed to deal with bullying (Chapter 10).

2   Divide and conquer

Children should never be questioned in groups—there is no advantage in this for all the reasons mentioned above. It must also be borne in mind that the bully will hide within a group if he is permitted to do so: he will use his unspoken power over the other members to prevent justice being done.

We have mentioned how individuals react differently when they are in groups; invariably, the inherent cohesiveness of a group makes the task of revealing the truth almost impossible. As soon as you suspect an episode of bullying, narrow down, in your mind, the group concerned as far as possible, and then immediately gather them together. Do not hesitate, or think that you can approach the matter in a piecemeal fashion. If you do, individuals will liaise and your task will become considerably more difficult.

When you have assembled the group, provide each of them with a pencil and paper and ask them to write down what they know of the issue. It is vital that you recruit a colleague to help here, for the pupils are now required to write in complete silence while you interview them individually in a separate room. If your colleague fails to keep absolute silence, he will be doing more harm than good because he will be destroying your credibility and enhancing the group's cohesiveness. So make sure that you choose a colleague who will not tolerate any nonsense.

From the personal interviews and the reports you will be able to detect any inconsistencies and begin to form a realistic picture of events.

Should the group be particularly small, it would be preferable to separate the individuals, but make sure that at all times they are being supervised and prevented from speaking to anyone until all of the interviews have been completed.

3　Individual investigative interviews

When you are interviewing each child as part of the preliminary investigations, try to create an atmosphere of confidentiality and trust.

Begin by asking him something that has nothing to do with the matter in hand: for instance, how the latest football match went. Or mention that you saw his name in the paper recently for his performance in an angling match. Try not to mention personal traits, and do not refer to his family. If the child is feeling apprehensive you will only make him more so, and less likely to tell you the truth. Your aim should be to relax him, to gain his trust.

State the confidential nature of your talk with him; mention how difficult it is to discuss things in front of others, but that you hope you may in the privacy of your room be able to resolve the matter. Make it clear that you did not witness the incident(s), and that he should not think that you are accusing him of being involved. What you are going to say is not directly related to the matter in hand, but you need to remind him in quite a general way that occasionally we all make mistakes and that when we do we often regret it. And in the case of bullying it can be very serious, because if parents become involved or the police are called in, then whoever is responsible for the incident could be taken to court.

You do not want this to happen, and you know that nobody else does. The child has many fine qualities and it would be in everyone's interest for any mistakes to be put right quickly, in this room, before the matter has to be handed over to higher authorities. Then ask him whether he understands what you are saying. Next, ask him to tell you what he knows about the issue, but to consider carefully what he is saying because all the others will be giving their views both in their personal interviews with you and in writing. He should then concentrate on the following questions:

1 When and where did the bullying take place?
2 Who was involved?
3 What part did you play?
4 How often did the bullying happen?
5 Who was (were) the victim(s)?
6 What happened to them? What form did the bullying take?
7 Did you do anything about it?
8 Who else knows about it?
9 Do your parents know about it?
10 Have you been involved in bullying before?

When each child has been interviewed, his statement should be cross-checked with what he has written. After the statements of all children have been considered, you should be able to say fairly accurately what has happened. When you are sure that you have discovered who did the bullying, who the victim was and what part she played, allow any other children to return to their normal activities.

4 Effective sanctions
Before you interview the bully, prepare a list of appropriate sanctions. Taking into account the nature of the bullying offence, make sure that whatever sanction you employ it will have sufficient impact to register with the bully, and an element of restitution.

In other words, whatever the punishment chosen, it will be harsh enough to have effect: the bullying must be associated with something unpleasant if the aggressor is to be deterred. Punishment in itself has this value: it clears the slate and allows children to make a fresh start. Second, the punishment should have some built-in positive element, in that it should offer the bully a way of putting things right. For example, if she has extorted money from another child she should pay it back, as well as having a sanction imposed upon her. If she has verbally humiliated someone she should receive a sanction and be made to write a letter of apology.

Appropriate sanctions will also be related to the bully's aptitudes and interests. If she is unable to carry out the punishment or if it would be a pleasure to her, it would be inappropriate.

5 Assets of bully and victim

Before beginning the interview with the bully, assess the good points that you can find in both bully and victim.

Always do this. It will place you in the right frame of mind as you approach the interview with the bully. If you can see her better side, perhaps your desire to hurt her will be tempered with a feeling that you are there to help. Also, you will find that whatever punishment you administer will not be *too* harsh, since you will be affirming it in her true interests. If you were in the frame of mind where you simply wanted to register your contempt and disgust, you would bully her.

So make a list of five positive aspects of her personality. Think of her leisure pursuits and personal interests; think of any special privileges that she holds in class (Chapter 5). Not only will this enable you to look upon her in a positive way, it will give you an indication of the kind of sanctions available to you.

Do the same with the victim. You will need to reassure her of her self-worth, so make sure that you know exactly what it is that you and others like about her.

Stage Two: The initial interview with the bully

1 Assume control

By the time you reach this stage, you know the identity of the bully. Your preliminary investigations have been thorough and you can now presume that, whatever she says, she may be twisting and turning to maintain some kind of credibility.

Adopt the same approach, therefore, that you took in Stage 1: help her to relax. Start by saying that the meeting is between the two of you at the moment, and it is important that the matter be resolved. You do not wish to involve people from outside the school unless absolutely necessary. Bullying is clearly against the rules; it is in no one's interests that it be tolerated. If she continues to intimidate and harass people, she could be dismissed; if the parents become involved she could be taken to court.

You are here to help her; she has made a mistake and it is important that the whole business is dealt with between the two of you in such a way that it will not happen again.

2 Assert the scenario

Tell her what the situation is as far as you can see it and as far as anyone else who examined the evidence would interpret it. Whatever the truth of the matter, this is the evidence: there is no doubt from this that she was bullying.

Do not mention the names of witnesses.

Do not allow her to intervene as you relate her involvement in as much detail as you can.

When you have finished, allow her to speak. Invite her to comment on what you have just stated.

When she has spoken, reaffirm the main points of the scenario; and unless there is a very serious doubt in your mind do not deviate from your original conclusions.

3 Assign punishment

You will have already made a list of suitable sanctions (p. 133). Tell the bully that you have decided that, to make amends, she will accept the following punishment. Let her know that, as she is being given a formal punishment, it will be recorded in your punishment book for private reference. Should she offend again, you would refer to the book when deciding what action to take.

Stage Three: The focused interview with the bully

When you have completed Stage 2 you will have firmly established what has happened and what punishment the bully will serve.

All the nasties have been completed! You must now reiterate what you have just said, but this time focus your conversation on the bully's needs. Remember that you are there to ensure that she will not merely complete her punishment and then carry on in her old ways. This is the part of the procedure where you will be digging deeper into the roots of her behaviour in an attempt to provide for her needs.

We discussed these in detail in Chapter 6. Here we will acknowledge them indirectly: her need to accept responsibility for her actions, to acknowledge the wrongness of bullying, to empathise with her victim; her need for a feeling of self-worth and her need to curb her impulsive and uninhibited behaviour.

So as you restate Stage 1 you should tackle the following five subjects.

1   The bully's responsibility for her own actions
You may now allow her to tell you what happened. In doing so she will invariably emphasise the part that others played in the episode. If she did bully it was because someone else wound her up or made her do it. She may have joined in because everyone else was doing it.

You must recognise here that she is desperately trying to save face. Do not attempt to stop her. When she has finished, say to her: 'Thank you for that account. What I want you to do now is to tell me the part that you played. Be honest about it. How did the episode start? What precisely did you say or do?'

Continue in this vein, never allowing her to relate what others did. She must say only exactly what part she played. If she does not accept that she played a part, tell her that as far as the episode goes the matter has been decided. Whatever she says now will not change anything. It is important at this stage for her to see what part she played, so that she does not get herself into the same kind of trouble again. There is always something that can be learned. Even a bystander could be asked why he did not go and get help. Ask her to reconsider the part that she played. What did she do or not do that was wrong?

Do not try to gain a confession of full responsibility. If

you focus on this, you will invariably drive her into a corner and she will confess nothing. Your skill *may* be such that you can gain a full confession, but if nothing much is forthcoming be content if you only get her to edge towards admitting responsibility. And if this *is* as far as you can get, make the general point that it is important to be able to admit responsibility for mistakes, and that it is a quality to be admired and a sign of strength.

2 The unacceptability of her behaviour

If the bully has admitted responsibility for her actions, concentrate now on getting her to appreciate why she behaved wrongly. If, on the other hand, she has admitted nothing, describe the action related in witness reports and continue to focus on the unacceptability of the behaviour.

Bear in mind that she may not be able to appreciate the moral and ethical reasons why her behaviour is wrong: she may only be able to look at the matter pragmatically. So adopt the following strategy:

a Think of the bully's precise behaviour. (Do not refer to bullying.)

b Ask her a moral/ethical question:

—Do you think that one person should be allowed to do this to another? (Mention the precise behaviour.)

c Ask her a pragmatic question:

—What might happen to someone who does this?

When she has answered make sure that you respond by reaffirming her correct responses, or by stating the correct responses for her. Say very clearly what you think about the unacceptability of the action. Say why it is ethically wrong and what would happen to a person who continually behaved like this.

3 Feelings

As already mentioned, bullies find it difficult to appreciate the feelings of their victims; they may find it difficult to feel anything themselves. So try to help her to empathise with the victim, and help her, too, to express her own feelings.

Ask her, for instance, to imagine herself as the victim and to relate the episode from the victim's point of view. If she cannot do this, ask her to imagine that she is the victim and put the following questions to her:

1 How did the incident begin?
2 What did you feel like?
3 Could you think of anything you might do?
4 Who were you scared of?
5 What do you feel should happen to the bully?

If she finds this difficult, you could pretend to be the victim and she could ask you the questions. Your replies should be full of feelings rather than thoughts. You are trying to get the bully to appreciate feelings rather than logic.

When the victim's feelings have been examined in this way, ask the bully:

1 How did you feel towards the victim before the incident occurred?
2 How did you feel when the bullying was taking place?
3 How did you feel when you knew that the matter was being investigated?
4 How did you feel when you thought that your parents or the police might be informed?
5 How do you feel now that the matter has been dealt with?

If she cannot do any of this, pretend to be her and allow her to ask you the questions. When you reply, again stress the feelings you might have had, rather than your thoughts.

4 Self-esteem

The bully may seem to have no problem with self-esteem—in fact, she may seem too full of herself. But whatever her self-esteem may appear to be, she will undoubtedly have a distorted perception of herself. However, if you have followed these proceedings she should be in a reasonably receptive frame of mind, so try to set aside any self-assuredness that she may have and take this opportunity to state:

what you like about her;
what her assets are;
how certain people rely on her (refer to your list on p. 134);
what her potential is;
how this might be realised.

Try to project a positive, likeable self-image on to her.

5   The unacceptability of her behaviour: punishment
Finally, restate the fact that it is because you know that she
is capable of being one of the best-behaved pupils that you
are disappointed with her behaviour. You like her and think
that she has a lot going for her. You are upset and saddened
when you see her letting herself down so badly.

You hope that when she has completed her punishment
it will be possible for her to make a fresh start and live up
to her full potential. Before you dismiss her:

—Ask her to state what her punishment is.
—Ask her to state why she is being punished.
—Tell her that everything that you have discussed is confidential: you will not talk about it to anyone else, and she
   will not mention the matter to her peers. Furthermore, if
   you receive the impression that she is treating the matter
   anything less than seriously, you will have to reconsider
   your approach and possibly refer the matter to the school
   principal.

Stage Four: The interview with the victim
When bullying occurs there is a tendency to deal with the
bully and presume that the victim will be all right.

This is wrong. The victim will usually have been suffering
from bullying for a considerable time; the incident that you
have dealt with will probably simply be the one that has
finally brought matters to breaking point. It may even be
that, because of the amount of pressure placed on her, the
victim has decided to provoke an incident that will be
noticed.

Whatever the situation, the victim's needs are paramount
and should be addressed as soon as the bully has been dealt
with. But she should not be interviewed as part of the in-

vestigative process (Stage 1); her involvement as the victim will have been established by others. See her after the investigative interviews and the interviews with the bully.

1 Reassurance

The victim will need to be reassured that she is safe and that she will no longer be threatened by the bully. You can provide her with this reassurance by telling her exactly what has happened. Tell her what your conclusions were, without mentioning the names of witnesses, and how the bully has been punished.

2 Responsibility

The victim will need to acknowledge exactly what happened before, during and after the incident, if she is to learn from it. Make sure that she is relaxed and comfortable in the knowledge that you are being in no way judgemental or condemnatory. Tell her clearly that you are asking her these questions in order to arrive at some way of avoiding problems in the future.

a Before the incident:
  —Where were you?
  —Who was with you?
  —What were you doing?

b During the incident:
  —What started things off?
  —Who was involved?
  —What did you do?

c After the incident:
  —What did you do?
  —Where did you go?
  —Who did you tell?

d Ask her these general questions:
  —Have there been other incidents?
  —Who was involved?
  —Did you tell anyone about these?

From the answers to all these questions you should be able to draw some conclusions and, more importantly, you should be able to make some recommendations. Use these further questions as a means of discussing the victim's responses:

a Before the incident:
—Do you think it was wise to be in that place at the time? Will you go there again?
—Do you think that it would have been better if you had been with another person?
—Do you think that whatever you were doing might have drawn the attention of the bully?

b During the incident:
  —Did you do anything that might have started the bully off?
  —When you saw the others involved in the incident approaching, did you feel that something was going to happen?
  —Did you do anything to avoid something happening? What do you think you could have done?

c After the incident:
  —After the incident started, what did you do? Do you think that you could have done anything to attract attention and help?
  —Where did you go after the incident? Where do you think you should immediately have gone?
  —Do you think that you should always tell someone when this kind of thing happens? Who do you think is the best person to see?

3 Rehearsal
When you have finished asking these questions, ask the child to summarise her conclusions; if she cannot, do it for her. You will need to rehearse possible techniques that she could use to avoid being bullied. Ask her to repeat:

—what she might do to avoid being bullied;
—what she might do to attract attention when she is being bullied;
—what she should do when she has been bullied.

Then consider what advice you might give to the child in terms of other strategies to be used. Your advice will depend on the nature of the bullying.

Physical bullying
If a child tries to retaliate physically, she will provide the bully with the reaction she is seeking. It is best for her to protect herself as well as possible and report the matter as soon as she can. However, if she is desperate and needs to take action, she should:

1   attract attention by making a lot of noise;
2   go for broke and hit hard;
3   escape;
4   report to the nearest adult;
5   report to parents or teacher.

Verbal bullying
The child should be told that if she reacts to teasing or taunts by losing her temper the bully will have won.

1   When verbal taunts are made she must think to herself: 'Poor bully. I can tell how weak she really is by what she is saying.'
2   She may choose to laugh with the bully and take a light-hearted approach to name-calling.
3   Ask her to tell you what people might tease her about. In this way you are trying to get her to appreciate that we all have peculiarities, and that it is when we can laugh about them that we are strong.
4   Tell the child that if she is ever threatened in any way, she should report the matter.
5   Stress the importance of episodes of racial and sexual harassment being reported immediately.

Extortion bullying
Persuade the child to avoid bringing a lot of possessions to school. Persuade her to be discreet about those possessions she does bring.

If the bully places her under any threat regarding favours to be performed, she should never give in unless her physical safety is threatened; she should report the threat as soon as possible.

Exclusion bullying
The child should be told to look to other groups for friendship. Explain to her that groups are temporary, that they change from time to time. The more she responds to being excluded the greater the pleasure of the bully.

Assure her that the matter will be dealt with. You could describe how this will happen: the group will be assembled and, without names being mentioned, the nastiness of exclusion bullying will be discussed. It will be made clear to the bully, without direct accusation, that her behaviour is noted. If after careful monitoring the bullying persists, the aggressor will be dealt with individually, in private (p. 134).

In all these matters you should stress to the victim the importance of her reporting all episodes of bullying; stress, too, that they will be dealt with in such a way that she will remain anonymous.

4 Feelings
If the victim is aware of her own feelings, she will feel more in control, and stronger. If she is aware of the bully's dynamics she may regard her as a person to be pitied rather than to be feared. In order to promote a greater awareness of the feelings involved in a bullying episode, you might ask her the following questions:

1 How did you feel when the incident occurred?
2 How did you feel afterwards?
3 How do you feel about the bully?
4 How do you feel about your performance?
5 Do you feel that you can talk to me or anyone else about your problems?

As a further exercise, you might like to ask her to role-play the bully. Ask her the following questions:

1 Why do you bully people?
2 What do you feel like inside?

3   Have you got any real friends?
4   Do you feel lonely?
5   Do you understand what your victims feel like?

If she cannot do this, you could play the bully and let her ask you the questions.

5   *Self-esteem*

The victim usually has a low self-esteem. Following an episode of bullying she will feel even more worthless. It is important that you reaffirm her worth in as many ways as possible.

Begin by stating that, although you have been looking at the ways in which she might avoid being bullied in the future, this in no way implies that she was responsible for the episode that has just happened. The bully was at fault, and she has been dealt with. It is important that ways of avoiding bullying are discussed because you care for her, as does everyone else, and you want her always to be safe and happy.

You can say why you like her and what her assets are (you listed them for this purpose, (p. 134). Say how happy you are that she is safe. Make sure that she knows what has been done about the matter, and tell her that everything you have mentioned is and will remain in complete confidence.

She should never hesitate to report matters to you in the future, even if she does not think they are important. You are there to listen to her and to help. Finally, make sure that she is aware of the school procedures with regard to bullying.

CONCLUSION

Episodes of bullying can vary enormously in terms of intensity and duration. In discussing bullying here, we are excluding the kind of mildly aggressive behaviour exhibited by most children as they learn to relate to each other and to control their emotions. Such behaviour is best treated with firm verbal condemnation. But participants should be regarded as neither victims nor bullies: they are simply children growing up and they need firm behaviour guidelines.

If we were to use the technique described in this chapter with every instance of aggression, we should have time for nothing else. Moreover, the technique would lose a considerable amount of its impact. It is when the behaviour is persistent and when the suffering by certain individuals becomes severe and sustained that we need to regard it as bullying and to investigate in the most thorough, yet private, fashion.

Although the procedure detailed above may seem cumbersome, in reality it should take no longer than fifteen minutes for the focused interview (p. 135). If it takes longer than this, little will register either with the bully or with the victim. It would be desirable, though, if both were offered the opportunity to receive more extensive counselling.

The provocative victim should be treated according to her particular condition, but in line with the treatment suggested for bullies and other victims. She would almost certainly require a programme of intensive therapy.

Apart from these techniques, teachers will be aware of behaviour modification programmes that may be employed with the bully. If they need further information on these, or on how they might deal with the underlying problems of the bully or the victim or both, they should consult their educational psychologist. In addition, they will have the support of the whole-school policy towards bullying, which should explain the agreed procedures for dealing with both bullies and victims. Part of this policy should describe the involvement of parents.

It is important for teachers to realise that unless they acquaint themselves and their children with these facilities they will have little chance of success with the more difficult cases.

9   What Parents Can Do

Parents who know that their child is involved in bullying will often feel at a loss when it comes to doing anything about it. They know that whatever action they take may have disastrous results: it could make the matter worse for their child, or it might destroy friendships they themselves have. If they report the matter to the school they may feel that they are taking the risk of looking foolish, over-protective and neurotic. As a result, they wait until the last moment before making a move.

This is understandable, but not at all appropriate. If they felt able to express their concerns, everyone would benefit: victims would not suffer and bullies would not assume undesirable behaviour patterns. Schools must take the initiative in this respect, and in Chapter 10 we shall be looking at the ways in which they can do this.

There are, though, things that parents can do on their own.

ASSESS YOUR CHILD

We have discussed how you might estimate whether your child has the characteristics of a bully or a victim (Chapter 1). Before you take any action, you must take it a stage further to determine whether or not he is involved in bullying.

Is my child bullying?
If he is bullying, you will probably hear from those close to him. If his brothers and sisters are suffering at his hands, you will hear their cries or you will notice their silence. You will know that something is going on.

The child may appear sullen and unhappy; he may have violent outbursts. He may suddenly have possessions of which you were unaware; he may not be able to account for all of his money. He may always appear to have sweets or different pens and pencils; he may always seem to be wearing someone else's coat.

If you notice that your child is acting differently, that he is beginning to swagger, that he is generally becoming more unapproachable and more unmanageable, and that he always seems to have more money than he should, you should link all this with any whispers and looks that may have been floating around and acknowledge that he may be bullying.

If people suddenly go quiet when you appear with your child, it could be that they want to say something about his behaviour that they cannot tell you without embarrassment. Be aware that no one is going to relish telling you that your child is a bully, and so you are the one who will have to take the initiative. It is important that you do not deny these indicators and that you take the necessary action.

Is my child being bullied?
If he is being bullied, he may be reluctant to go to school. He may have stomach pains or headaches, or feel nauseous: he will use any excuse not to attend. He may be unable to explain why some of his belongings are missing; he may have strange excuses for the state of his clothing, or the fact that he has, for example, lost one of his shoes. He may begin to wet the bed or to stammer; he may stop eating; he may have nightmares.

He may appear always to need money to take to school: he may steal this from you. If he becomes withdrawn and quiet, or suddenly starts to lash out and tries to explain this behaviour with excuses that are clearly prefabricated, you can assume that there is a good possibility that he is being bullied.

But he will be very reluctant to admit it, and so you should be prepared to investigate the matter from other directions.

ASSESS YOUR SITUATION

Before you take any form of direct action, it would be
wise to take one last look at the possibility of there being a
simple reason for your child's behaviour. We mentioned in
Chapter 1 that there are a number of common reasons for
poor behaviour.

Family problems

Children are particularly sensitive to change and to stressful
relationships. Examine the situation in your immediate
family and see whether there are any factors that might have
coincided with the onset of his behavioural difficulties. Here
are some questions you should ask:

Changes
1   Has a member of the family recently left home?
2   Has a new member arrived?
3   Has there been a bereavement in the family?
4   Has the family recently moved house?
5   Have there been any other significant changes?

Relationships
6   Have you and your spouse started to argue a lot?
7   When did your relationship with him/her change?
8   Have your other children been particularly difficult?
9   Do you feel that you ignore your child too much?
10 Do you expect too much of him?

Circumstances
11 Have you had problems with the neighbours?
12 Do you have relatives or someone else to talk to?
13 Have you had financial problems?
14 Have you had health problems?
15 What lies ahead for you?

In answering these questions you will have aired both facts
and feelings that may have caused your child's behaviour to
deteriorate.

ASSESS YOUR FEELINGS

Feeling responsible

You must not blame yourself for your child's behaviour. We are all born into this world with our own personality, and we all react differently to life circumstances. Your child will have had to contend with the circumstances of your life, but do remember that none of us can exist in a vacuum: when we are born we all enter the lives of other people. It is our own personality that determines how we cope.

After answering these questions you may have been able to think of ways in which you can make it easier for your child to cope, and this is as much as you can do. In Chapter 1 we discussed how he might have the tendencies of a bully or of a victim; your responsibility as a parent is to assess this and then provide the right kind of setting. It is not easy, since until a child begins to behave badly we are unaware that something needs to be done.

Feeling desperate

If you feel that nothing can be done about your child's situation, you are wrong. (We shall be discussing the action you can take later in the chapter (p. 159).) And if you feel that nothing can be done about your own situation, you are equally wrong.

A good analogy is to think of yourself as an automatic jukebox. You are in charge, and you can play whatever record you like. If you want to be bright and cheerful, you can; if you want to be miserable, just press the right button. No one presses the buttons for you! People suffer from despair usually because they think they should be doing something else or being different in some way; when they despair of their child, they have a picture of how he or she should be behaving or achieving. It is useful regularly to overhaul your ideal model. (p. 56).

Never despair for your child: accept him whether he is a bully or a victim. Take whatever action needs to be taken, and acknowledge that you are in a position to help. Whatever you do will, at the very least, let him know that you care. You may think that by interfering you will make matters worse. But reframe your thoughts: do not think that you are interfering—think of yourself as *intervening*. Those who interfere usually spoil things for others, but you will be trying to do the opposite.

SHARE YOUR CONCERNS

You will find it invaluable if you are able to share your concerns with someone.

Neighbours and other significant adults

If you have a friendly neighbour whose opinions you respect, explain to her your worries about your child's behaviour. Ask her whether she thinks you have got everything wrong. Very often a person outside the family will see things differently. If you make it clear to your neighbour that you would very much appreciate an honest opinion, you might be surprised at the view she offers.

She may feel that you are over-reacting to his behaviour. Or she may confirm what you think and express similar concerns, adding that she has had them for a long time but has not liked to say anything. Whatever she says, she may well help you to put things in perspective and be able to provide you with a more accurate picture of your child's behaviour. As an added bonus, you may find that by being honest with your neighbour you have initiated a supportive friendship.

Your child, too, needs other adults to talk to. If he has others to whom he can turn, he may be able to resolve many of his problems. Unless there is another adult who will listen to his feelings, he is in no position to express how he feels about those closest to him. You may have relatives outside your immediate family, or friends, who can help in this way. Children usually have a favourite uncle or aunt.

If it is possible to arrange for your child to stay with a relative regularly, you will be able to have a rest and he will acquire another listening ear, especially if you have discussed your concerns about his behaviour with his host beforehand. And if he behaves well with other adults, do not be envious. Be pleased about it! We all act differently with people whom we know less well. His improved behaviour does not mean that he loves them more than he loves you.

Other adults such as youth leaders, priests and sports coaches can serve the same purpose: in this respect, and with regard to improving your child's self-image, it is very important for him to belong to interest groups outside the home.

Brothers and sisters
Express your concern about his behaviour to your other children. Brothers and sisters will often know a lot more about a child's behaviour than his parents do. They may, however, have decided to honour a vow of secrecy with the victim, or may have been threatened with reprisals by the bully.

You can encourage them to talk by speaking freely to them about some of your minor personal problems (judiciously chosen). Later, when you have the opportunity and they are used to discussing feelings with you, you might feel able to ask how they feel about their brother's behaviour. In this way you may acquire confirmation that he is either bullying or being bullied.

In general terms, encourage your children to:

1   Tell you when one of them is having difficulties. Impress upon them that you are there to help. All children have problems from time to time, and unless they let their parents know they cannot help.
2   Tell their teacher, if they feel that they cannot tell you. You will respect them for taking this form of action, and will not be angry that they have been unable to tell you first.

If you cultivate an atmosphere where your children feel that it is safe to talk about feelings, you may find that the bully or the victim himself will talk to you.

TALK TO THE BULLY

Special times
Make the effort to talk to your child if you think he is bullying. In addition to spontaneous chats when the moment arises, make a special time available each week. But don't

just sit and talk—do something and talk. Take the dog for a long walk together, or clear the garden. Begin by talking about nothing in particular (such as sport or TV), and aim after a few sessions to reach the point where you can begin to discuss feelings and relationships.

Say how enjoyable you have found it going for walks and having a chat; how everyone needs someone to talk to, especially when they have things on their mind. Ask the child if *he* has anyone like this. If not, you could suggest yourself; if you feel unhappy with this, that it is not a realistic proposition, suggest someone else. Tell him who *you* talk to when you are worried, and how you would like to feel that you could also tell him things. Add that you are glad that he could listen to you today.

Repeat this general kind of conversation, revealing a few of your own problems each time.

Topics of conversation
In a later conversation, when you feel that you have his confidence, you could raise certain issues relating to bullying. He may suggest that some of the situations apply to him, or he may just listen and absorb what you are saying.

Do not insist on talking about these situations, though, and don't broach the problem of his bullying with him. (We will be discussing how to tackle that in a more direct way later.) Here you are simply trying to present him with an opportunity to do two things:

1   to talk to you and tell you about his bullying and why it might be happening;
2   to listen to your unequivocal views on what is right and what is wrong.

The situations to present are these:

1   Leadership and bullying
Your child may boss others about because he thinks this is a sign of leadership. He may have been encouraged to think or feel that people are important when they throw their weight around. He may not be able to appreciate the difference between being a leader and being a bully.

Ask him what he thinks the difference is. If he cannot answer, or won't, tell him that a leader helps others less fortunate than himself by showing them what to do and inspiring them to achieve their objectives by his good example. A bully, on the other hand, uses others for his enjoyment, making them do things that they do not want to do and gaining pleasure by seeing them suffer.

Encourage him to give examples of people who act in this way; if he does, you can then develop the theme in terms of any hero that he may have. He will find it easier to talk about the evil machinations of some hero rather than directly reveal himself to you. The hero could be a fantasy figure, or a person in real life whom he admires.

When he is relating examples of bad behaviour, bear in mind that he could be telling you about himself. But do not confront him with this. Allow him to expand his thoughts and to discuss the behaviour from outside himself. As you join in his fantasies, remember that you are trying to get him to appreciate that bullying is not to be admired and that it is good to help others in a kind and considerate way.

2   Individuals and groups

Your child may not be able to appreciate why some children play in groups and why others find it difficult. He may feel frustrated that he cannot make friends. So explain to him that some children play on their own because they like to, and that others simply prefer to play in groups. Most children sometimes play in groups and sometimes on their own, depending on what they feel like.

Say that there are some children who do not like sharing their friends, and that if a new child comes along they may push him away and make sure that no one has anything to do with him. Tell him that this is wrong; if he were the new child, he would not like it.

Ask him if he has ever been unhappy because he was not in a group. Which children would he have in *his* group and which would he not have? You might suggest that if he were to invite those children who were not in his group to join him, he would be like a true leader because he would be helping others and showing them how to have a good time.

A vital point to make is that when you do things on your own you can do what you want, but if you are a member of a group you have to do what the group wants. If he wants to be in a group, he will at first have to be quiet and do what the rest want to do. After he has made friends with them they will listen to whatever he may suggest. But they won't listen if he is bossy and tries to push them about.

3 Being bullied

You might discuss what it feels like to be pushed around by someone bigger than yourself; you might talk about being frightened by others. Tell your child that it is wrong for those who feel that they are strong to bully others. If you are strong, you should help those who are weak. A big strong boy should be kind and gentle; if he is not, people will say that he is a bully and will not like him.

Ask him whether he has ever been bullied and whether he can remember what it was like. Does he know of anybody at school who is bullied, and could he imagine being in their place?

Tell him that if a person makes serious threats to a boy or girl, if he takes things away from them or makes them do things they do not want to, or if he physically assaults anyone, that person can be reported to the police and taken to court. Bullying is a very serious offence.

During these conversations your bullying child may reveal his feelings and thoughts to you, especially if you have progressed slowly and built upon his trust. Or he may say nothing. However, his body language may tell you that he is more relaxed and at ease with himself.

In any case, he will have listened to you expressing your feelings and will have heard your thoughts. He will have absorbed all of this, and although his behaviour may not change immediately, he may use what you have said later— even if it is not until he is telling his own children how to behave! (Have you noticed how like your own parents you become as you get older?)

To see an immediate change in his behaviour you will undoubtedly have to employ other techniques (p. 162), but these will have little lasting effect unless you have created a genuine shift in his attitude. This will take a long time, but in your walks and conversations you have already initiated the process.

TALK TO THE VICTIM

Special times
You will already have arranged for your child to attend a club or association, and this will introduce him to another set of adults. It will help him to separate from you (Chapter 7) and to begin to assume his own identity, and it will also help him generally to relate to people—in particular to cope with the more domineering type of person. If you have been attending the organisation with him, make sure that you stop doing so as soon as possible. You are trying to introduce him to a life of his own, so let go at the earliest opportunity.

This does not mean that you need never spend time on your own with him. On the contrary, it is important that you do so. Even if you feel that you relate well with your child and that there are many opportunities for him to speak to you, you should allocate a special time for being with him. Try to arrange to do something together rather than just sitting and talking. The reason you give him for being together could be to take the dog for a walk, or simply that you need the exercise.

When you are with him, remember that the purpose of this special time is to allow him to speak. You are not spending time with him specifically to discuss bullying. This may come later, but for the moment concentrate on encouraging him to express his thoughts and feelings, which you can do in the following ways:

1 Express your own thoughts and feelings
In order to achieve a response from him, be careful how you project yourself. Do not be dogmatic and overbearing; do not make bold statements; do not try to be clever.

Instead, speak quietly and ask open ended questions;

show a genuine interest in what you are saying. Talk about matters that concern you, but that are not related to your child's problem. For instance, discuss the poor bus service to town, or the fact that the postman never seems to deliver the mail on time. Do not burden him with any serious problems you may have. Your child is unable to cope with his own difficulties, and you would be placing him under enormous pressure if you were to tell him of any major family or personal crises relating to health, finance or relationships.

2   Listen to your child's response

He may reply, or he may not. If he does reply, listen carefully. Indicate, by the odd comment, that you are interested; and encourage him to talk by asking more questions. Do not make a judgement on what he says. If he says nothing and appears uninterested, bear in mind that he will still be listening to what you say. At some point say how nice it is to have someone to talk to.

When you feel that the time is right (but it would be fatal to rush into this), you can introduce into your conversation certain topics that relate to bullying.

Topics of conversation

1   Coping

Tell your child of the fond memories you have of your own school. Describe your favourite teachers and lessons; tell him of things you did with other children whom you liked. The point is to give him the impression that there were good times at school.

Then let him know that there were some subjects that you hated, and some teachers whom you disliked. There were also children who could be nasty at times. Some would push others around; they would take such things as pens and pencils from them. You remember how one boy even pulled a pair of trainers off another and refused to give them back. If the boy complained, he said, he would beat him up after school. You wonder what has happened to these people . . . You remember being pushed around yourself when you were at school, and being frightened of one boy in particular.

You used to feel scared whenever he came near you, and you know that other children used to feel the same.

You think that it is wrong for such a child to be allowed to make others so unhappy. The boy needed to be reported so that it could all stop. If it *had* been reported, they could all have relaxed and he could have been helped.

When you were at school everyone had to put up with that boy. There was no one to tell; no one would listen. You and your friends used to feel terrible, scared to go to school . . . You used to think that there was something wrong with you . . . but now you realise that it wasn't you—it was him. At the time you felt that you just had to cope on your own, that nothing could be done about it.

2 Responding

Tell your child of things that annoy you. Describe in a light-hearted way how your partner will never eat crusts; how his grandmother will insist on cutting carrots lengthways; how the newspaper boy often delivers the wrong papers on a Sunday morning. The one thing that really annoys you is when people call you Vi instead of Vivienne. You can't stand it! You are sure that they do it deliberately, just to annoy you.

You remember that when you were at school children used often to call people names, just to see what they would do. There was one boy called David Cabbage, who used to get teased a lot. (Guess why!) At first he used to shout and cry—and everyone knew that he would do this. There was one boy in the class who used to deliberately call him names, in a whisper, when the teacher couldn't hear, and David used to get so annoyed that he would leap out of his desk and try to attack this boy, who was a giant compared to him. It was funny to watch, for you and your friends, but not for David. Anyhow, he got so fed up that eventually he simply stopped responding. It was the best thing he ever did. You remember him when he was a bit older, simply laughing when someone called him a name. It didn't bother him any more. Even though he had a funny name people just stopped teasing him, because there was no point, they only made themselves look foolish . . .

Then talk about nicknames—what you were called, what the teachers were called. Have a good laugh about it all!

3 Telling

Think of a genuine situation in your life when you were so worried that you eventually told someone about the problem. If possible, think of an episode of bullying, but don't choose one that involved your child or anyone he knows. If possible, take an example from your own schooldays when you were under pressure from another pupil or pupils.

Describe how you felt before you told. Tell him why you were frightened to tell anyone, why you couldn't talk to certain people, and why you eventually chose the person you did. Describe what happened when you plucked up courage, and how you felt when that person listened to you.

Make the following points:

1   We are all afraid to tell anyone when we are worried; we feel sure that it is better to keep troubles to ourselves.
2   We often feel that nothing can be done; we think that no one can help.
3   We feel that it is wrong to tell tales about others.

Emphasise your response to these feelings in this way:

1   It is much better to tell someone about our problems; if we do, they seem to disappear or at least diminish.
2   If you do not tell anyone, nothing can be done; if you do tell someone, they may be able to help, and if they can't they will find someone who can.
3   If someone is doing something wrong, then you will help him or her and everybody else by telling someone. If you do not tell, you are as guilty as he or she is.

By sharing your thoughts and feelings in this way, and by centring them on these topics of conversation, you may find that your child begins to talk to you. He may even begin to discuss the bullying in which he is involved.

Do not rush this process; you must see these special times and conversations as being the main thrust of the long-term work to be undertaken with him.

Whether your child could be considered a passive victim, a provocative victim or a bully, he will benefit from the reassurance that these focused sessions of caring offer him. But you will also need to take more direct action, and it is to this that we will now give our attention.

TAKE ACTION

A If your child is a victim

1 Speak to his school
When your child is being bullied, it is nearly always best to deal with the matter through the school. This saves embarrassment for the child and may preserve your friendships. As we have noted, schools are aware that bullying occurs and many have devised strategies to prevent it happening. Parents can help by reporting episodes of bullying in as much detail as possible. The first person to see is usually the class teacher. But before you see her make sure you can answer the following questions in relation to the alleged bullying:

1 What has happened to your child?
2 How often has this happened?
3 Who is responsible?
4 When did the bullying take place?
5 Where did it take place?
6 Did your child report it?
7 To whom was it reported?
8 Who told you about the bullying?
9 What are the signs that make you believe something is definitely going on?
10 Is your child anxious about anything else?

Armed with this information, the class teacher may then instigate an investigation and deal with the bully (Chapter 8). She may proceed with other techniques or procedures installed within the whole-school anti-bullying policy (Chapter 10).

If you are not happy with the response you receive when you discuss the matter with the class teacher, ask to see the head. If you are not happy with *his* response, write and inform him that you are going to approach the school governors. You will be providing them with details of your child's difficulties and an account of the response that you have so far received from the school. You will also be asking them to provide you with a copy of the whole-school anti-bullying policy.

It is not often necessary to take such measures: most schools welcome parents and want to work in partnership with them. Do not hesitate, therefore, to contact the class teacher whenever you are concerned about your child; invariably, your information will prove to be of valuable assistance. The teacher may have been perplexed by his behaviour for some time, and unable to detect the underlying reason. If she is a good teacher, she will welcome you with open arms. Together you should decide:

1   what will now happen to the bully;
2   what you might do to help your child at school and at home.

2   Speak to the bully's parents

If you live in a close community and know the parents of the bully, speak to them before approaching the school. They might resent it if you were to go directly to your child's teacher and make formal complaints.

Although you know the parents, you should still bear in mind the sensitive nature of the subject; you could still cause bad feelings if you approached it too directly. If you know them really well, simply say that you think there is trouble between the children; it looks to you as though their child is being too heavy with yours. But if you don't know the parents so well, begin by saying that you feel that something is going on between your children; you are not too sure what it is, but you wonder whether they have noticed anything. Your child tends to look sheepish when he comes off the school bus these days. Also, he is reluctant to go to school— a complete change from the days when he couldn't wait to get there . . . It does look at though the two have been fighting or arguing . . . has their son said anything to them?

The conversation may drift into some agreement, or it may not. In any event, you will have broached the matter.

Making them aware of the possibilities may be enough to ensure that they speak to their son.

Remember not to make any definite statements or allegations. Your aim is to create a situation where, as mature adults, you may together resolve the matter.

3 Speak to the bully

As we noted earlier, the inclination of most parents who discover that their child is being bullied is to meet the bully and give him a taste of his own medicine.

This is an understandable reaction, but it is one that has been proved to have no long-term beneficial effect: when physical violence is inflicted on children, they tend to do the same to others. By beating a child you will be promoting violence in him, and others will suffer at his hands. You may feel that by doing so you would deter him from behaving in this way, but in reality any change in his behaviour would be short-lived. The only permanent effect could be the acquisition of a criminal record—by you! No matter what you feel like doing, be aware that you are not allowed by law to assault anyone, never mind children.

You may, though, achieve something by meeting the bully and telling him exactly what you know about his behaviour. But remain calm when you do so. Do not shout. Quietly tell him that if he persists in bullying your child you will approach his parents, contact his headmaster and if necessary report him to the police.

Tell him not to mention this conversation to your child, and to keep away from him. If you hear that there have been any other incidents you will not hesitate to take the action you have just outlined.

Do not use swear words or threats—they may be held against you. Simply tell him what will happen if he persists with his behaviour.

4 Speak to your child

When it is clear that your child is being bullied, make sure that you talk to him in detail about it, and devise some strategies that he can employ. A suggested procedure can be found in Chapter 8.

B If your child is a bully

1 *Speak to his school*
Before you speak to your child, discuss your fears and concerns with his teacher. When you go to the school take with you the answers to these questions:

1   Who is he bullying?
2   What does he do to them?
3   When does it happen?
4   Where does it happen?
5   Are other children involved?
6   How long has this been going on?
7   How did you get to know about it?
8   Has anyone reported it to the school?
9   Why do you feel that he could be bullying?
10 Do you suspect that he is involved in other things?

Do not hesitate to ask for a private discussion. The teacher will welcome your cooperation and respect you for bringing the matter to her attention. She will tell you what will happen next as far as the school is concerned. Together you should decide what might be the best approach for you to take at home.

This really is a matter on which agreement is needed. If the child were to be severely punished at school, it would not be wise to double it by repeating it at home: punishment can be counter-productive if it is too harsh. Neither would it be wise for you to repeat the investigation techniques of the teacher (Chapter 8).

When your child is bullying, it is essential that your first step be to approach the school.

2 *Speak to your child*
After speaking to the school about his bullying behaviour, speak to him. Be clear about your facts and be quietly determined to assert the situation as you see it. If the school has not got the time to interview him or to help him by discussing the details of his bullying, you should do this. In the focused interview (p. 135) you will find a suggested outline for an interview/discussion.

Although the school should have imposed some sanctions on him, you too should affirm your strong disapproval of his behaviour by imposing some of your own (Chapter 5). But make sure that these are balanced against those already imposed by the school.

If you are not happy with the response you receive from the school, follow the procedure suggested on p. 159.

CONCLUSION

Although there is a great deal that parents can do by spending time with their difficult child and by encouraging him to share his thoughts and feelings, they must never hesitate to seek help. Neighbours and other members of the family may present an alternative perspective for them. They should not forget that others can listen and understand.

An increasing number of professionals have been trained to recognise and deal with bullies and victims. If their battle against bullying is to succeed, they need parents to provide them with information. They need to work with them to devise efficient procedures, to create effective deterrents and to implement appropriate personal treatment programmes.

If your child is a bully or a victim, and whether his problems are great or small, you will need to consult your family and friends; above all, you will need to contact his school. Never hesitate to do so.

In the next chapter we will look at some of the ways in which schools try to combat bullying; if you have suggestions of your own get involved and take them to the Parent–Teacher Association (PTA) meetings.

Recognise that your child's school belongs to you: it is one of your many responsibilities to see that all children who attend are protected from bullying.

10 What Schools Can Do: An Anti-bullying Policy

It will be clear by now that, if bullying is to be stopped, then parents, schools and other agencies must work together to provide a systematic, comprehensive and sustained anti-bullying programme. While bullying episodes can be dealt with on an individual basis, a crisis-management approach will do nothing to solve the problem in the long term. Neither will it be addressing the fact that most bullying takes place in secret and is never reported.

It is in schools that we can combat the problem, for it is here that we can research where and when bullying takes place, and who does it. With this information, we can begin to implement effective strategies. So it is schools in conjunction with parents who should take the initiative and devise anti-bullying policies, and in doing so they should consider the following matters.

ASSESSMENT

A good way to begin devising an anti-bullying policy is for you, the teacher, to discover as much as you can about the bullying that is taking place in your school. It would be extremely useful to know how much of it is going on, what is actually happening, where it is happening and who is doing it to whom. This may seem a daunting task, but all the information can be acquired by simply asking the children.

Special questionnaires designed by experts are available for this purpose (Appendix B). It is better to use these rather than to devise your own, because they must be the right length, be unambiguous and avoid offending those who complete them.

Issuing the questionnaire at the beginning of your anti-bullying campaign will in itself raise awareness. So it would be wise to seize the opportunity and prepare preliminary material to be used with the children either before the questionnaire, to heighten its effect, or afterwards to capitalise on the interest it may generate. It is worth mentioning that after the first stage of your campaign there will appear to be a surge of bullying: this should be interpreted as an indication of the success of your initiative—the children have started to report.

INDUCTION PROCEDURES

A great deal of bullying occurs when children start a new school, whether infant school or secondary school. Therefore, before they start a new school they and their parents should attend a series of induction meetings. These meetings are particularly useful for prospective entrants to secondary school, where the greatest amount of bullying occurs.

At these meetings the children can become familiar with the surroundings, and both they and their parents can be made aware of school procedures and expectations. The school should make it clear to parents that it welcomes their views and comments at all times, and that the successful implementation of the policies relies on parents and school working together. In particular, the policies relating to behaviour, discipline and bullying need the full support of the parents. Regular PTA meetings should be held in order that teachers and parents may keep the policies under constant review. Whenever policy meetings are to be held, parents must attend—this requirement should be stated as a firm condition of enrolment.

During the induction procedure the following statements relating to bullying should be presented for discussion.

1 A code of conduct for parents
1 Parents will attend PTA meetings. Attendance at designated policy meetings will be mandatory.
2 Parents will be supplied with information regarding bullying and what to do about it, and will not hesitate to report any suspicions to the class teacher.

3 Parents will recognise the genuine concern of teachers for their child, and will welcome any information regarding the involvement of their child in bullying.

4 Parents will be prepared to devise and implement, with the class teacher, a plan of action that may be carried out regarding the involvement of their child in bullying. The plan would relate to action that would be taken by both the teacher and the parent.

5 Parents will, when in the presence of their child, fully support any policy decisions relating to behaviour, discipline and bullying; if they need to question decisions, this will be done privately with the class teacher.

2   A code of conduct for teachers

1   Teachers will always contact parents when they have any concern regarding the behaviour of a child.

2   Teachers will acknowledge and respect the unique perspective that both they and the parents hold.

3   Teachers will acknowledge the unique stressors under which both they and the parents deal with the child.

4   Teachers will respect the need for confidentiality when they are dealing with parents or children who are involved in bullying.

5   Teachers will acknowledge the importance of the parent–teacher partnership; they will particularly recognise the needs of those parents whose children are involved in bullying.

3   A code of conduct for children

This should be precise and detailed, rather than a vague suggestion that children should behave well and avoid being bullied. Remember that in this book only the elements relating to bullying are mentioned—a full code of conduct outlining the school's expectations regarding behaviour in the classroom and around the school would normally be presented. The following are essential points for children to remember:

1   They should tell their class teacher or their parents when they are unhappy about anything.

2   They should find a private time and report bullies to

the class teacher; if they do this they will be helping other children, and will be praised.

3   They should tell their parents when nothing seems to be being done about bad behaviour or bullying.

4   They should always walk to and from school with a friend, and should vary the route that they take. If they are unhappy about travelling on the school bus they should tell their class teacher or parent.

5   They should not take toys and other belongings to school; they should take food only when they need a packed lunch; money should never be taken unless the school has requested it.

6   They should stay within sight of staff; they should avoid those parts of the school where there are few people, especially during breaktimes.

THE ROLE OF PARENTS AND OTHER SIGNIFICANT ADULTS

When schools have been able to support and help parents, the behavioural problems presented by their children have diminished considerably.

Schools should not adopt the attitude that they are the experts and that they can teach parents how to raise their children. This approach is disrespectful and based on ignorance. It will do nothing to promote a working relationship with parents, and will only result in an escalation of the behavioural difficulties being experienced by their children.

Schools should acknowledge that many parents need only to know that there is somebody who understands what they are going through with their child, somebody who will simply listen to them rather than lecture them. When they are offered this listening ear they may become strong enough in themselves to begin to assert control over their child. PTA meetings may be too formal for many parents. Although mandatory attendance at policy meetings should stand, teachers could arrange informal coffee sessions for parents who need to meet on a more casual basis. Parents may find it easier on these occasions to chat about anything they do not understand, or about any problems that they may have.

The human relations specialist (p. 176) would have a specific responsibility to work with parents in this way.

As part of their anti-bullying policy schools and parents should recognise the value of their having strong links with other local organisations. Both bullies and victims can benefit enormously by being involved in external clubs and societies, but very often they and their parents find it difficult to make the initial contact.

A list of local organisations should be compiled and representatives contacted. They should be invited to give talks at PTA meetings, and the school should tell them of its programme relating to bullying, which would include a deliberate policy of introducing those children who were experiencing difficulties into local organisations.

Shopkeepers, traffic wardens, library workers and anyone else who lives or works in the vicinity of the school should be invited in and made to feel part of it. They could be invited for coffee and biscuits on a special evening once a year, perhaps when the new intake is paying a preliminary visit, and told of the school's policy towards bullying and other unacceptable behaviour. Teachers could inspire them with stories of their counterparts in New Zealand and Australia, who have proved to be effective allies in this respect.

NURSERY SCHOOLS

Special consideration should be given to the impact that good nursery education has on the incidence of bullying and antisocial behaviour at a later age.

Bullying may begin in nursery school, so when children meet and interact with others for the first time it is extremely important that their behaviour be closely observed. When bullying is ignored at this age it achieves great significance. The aggressor thinks it is acceptable, and the victim becomes fearful of others and learns to be passive.

If a child begins to bully, the teacher should take her to one side and firmly say that she should not behave like this. She should then concentrate on preventing her from repeating the behaviour: before she has a chance to bully, the teacher should deflect her into another activity. She should also concentrate on praising the child whenever she is behaving well. She may give her rewards: an appropriate one would be a smile and a friendly comment, although more tangible rewards such as stars or small toys may be given.

Those who work in nursery schools should have a knowledge of such behaviour modification techniques and of early childhood development. They should know how to introduce children to pre-reading and number work, and be trained in promoting communication and negotiation skills. Above all, they should have the capacity to project warmth and to empathise with very young children.

Many children become involved in bullying because of learning difficulties. In nursery schools these can be observed and the children can be given extra help; the information can then be passed to the infant school that they are to attend.

Nursery schools need to forge strong links with local schools, and children and their parents should pay several visits to the infant school before they start attending. The parents of a child who is experiencing major problems in nursery school should be encouraged to discuss any difficulties they may have at home, and they can join with the teacher in preparing a child care plan which would incorporate what might be done in the home and at school to minimise future difficulties.

If, at any time, severe problems are anticipated, they should seek the advice of their educational psychologist.

Although bullying does occur in nursery schools, when it is observed and controlled it has little detrimental effect—the advantages of attending more than compensate for the risk involved. The child who has a tendency to dominate others will learn how to interact with them in an appropriate way: the child who tends to be passive will learn to cope with those who are more aggressive.

It has been observed that in those countries where children receive nursery education there is a noticeable decrease in the incidence of violence and crime at a later age. However, it is not simply the existence of such facilities that has this desirable effect: to be effective, they must provide a structured and stimulating educational setting.

BOARDING SCHOOLS

Children in boarding schools cannot retreat to the safety of their homes in the evening. So it is extremely important that there be a clearly outlined reporting system for them to use.

Apart from measures which all schools should introduce and which are mentioned elsewhere, boarding schools should arrange for a person who is independent of the school to be the contact point for any child who wishes to speak in confidence about bullying or any other matter. To facilitate this, children should have access to a private telephone line. The procedure should be clearly explained to them, and details of it should be displayed near the telephone.

Boarding schools have an extra responsibility to children who are away from their parents, and they must make a special effort to clarify procedures and to deal firmly with any episodes of bullying. Children sleeping at school need to feel safe: they need added assurances that such behaviour will not be tolerated.

TROUBLE SPOTS

There are certain times during the school day when large numbers of children of mixed ages gather together in unstructured and poorly supervised groups. It is mainly at these times that bullying occurs. When the school and parents are considering anti-bullying policies it is important for them to consider the particular problems that may occur at these times.

Going to and from school

The first and last times of the day when problems may arise are when children are going to school and returning home. Some walk or cycle. Others travel on school buses, where supervision may be non-existent if one acknowledges that the driver is in no position to supervise anyone.

There are solutions. In addition to the driver, there should always be at least one responsible adult on the bus. This person should be included on in-service training programmes, and his brief should be to ensure that every pupil on the bus is safe and free from any form of harassment. If money is not available for this purpose, the Parent–Teacher Association should be approached for a group of volunteers. Parents should also be advised to tell children who make their own way to school to vary the route.

Many problems arise when pupils are waiting for school transport, particularly when they are delayed at the departure point. The problems here are usually the result of a minimum number of staff being allocated to the departure point, and the other teachers sending their children to meet them there. A simple solution would be for each teacher to take his group to the bus point, and those who needed to depart on foot could be dismissed from there. A member of staff should also be assigned to supervise any pupils who leave from the cycle shed.

The school needs also to consider the fact that bullying often involves an older pupil picking on a younger one: to avoid this, the times of arrival and departure can be staggered for the different year groups.

Such rearrangements can be simply thought out and implemented. The school needs to recognise that for many children, getting to school and getting home are experiences that keep them awake at night. It is not until they are in the classroom that they feel safe.

Breaktimes
Children are bullied most in the playground. This is the time when, in many schools, the old-fashioned teacher's break is still mandatory. As a result, hordes of children are placed in a confined space, usually with nothing to do and effectively with no one in charge of them. The obvious solution is to make playtimes as flexible as possible. In infant and junior schools this should pose few problems: class teachers can be given discretion to either have breaks or not have them, and to have them in a choice of places. They should be provided with refreshments in their own classroom (as should the children).

Whenever mass gatherings of children are avoided, the potential for bullying is minimised. Teachers who have the flexi-break option can use breaks as incentives, which gives them the added advantage of being able, when appropriate, to cancel them as a sanction. In fact, if they are teaching well and their children have a variety of things to do, there is no reason why the children should need a morning or an afternoon break. Toilet breaks can be taken individually— so long as this is interpreted literally.

Lunchtimes, in particular, can cause enormous problems for those staff who are appointed to make the token gesture of 'being in charge'. The trouble is that the problems that arise then are taken back into the school for the afternoon session.

If breaktimes are to be held for any particular group they should be discreetly organised. Pupils may be taken on to the yard for a game of softball, or allowed to relax in the classroom. The teacher will have foreseen any potential problem combinations of children, and either subtly directed them apart or placed herself close to them. The classroom should be equipped for the purpose, with a variety of things for children to do; likewise, the playground should be designed to encourage them to play constructively.

Staff should have carefully planned facilities and procedures for these times; they should prefer in their own interest and in that of their pupils to commit themselves to a short game of football or a game of draughts rather than to promote behavioural difficulties by sitting in the staff room drinking tea and dreading the first period in the afternoon, or their particular dinner duty day.

Recent experience has shown that when playgrounds are made into soft environments where children can be stimulated by a variety of attractive equipment, their behaviour becomes less aggressive. If the playground is well designed it will allow them to play on their own, with another person or in larger groups. They will be able to practise their fine and gross motor skills, or indulge in private and useful fantasy. Secondary school play areas should also be purposefully designed, with opportunities for team ball games and racquet games, and areas for private study.

Equally important, at both junior and senior level, is the notion of children remaining only with their age group (see p. 174). The flexi-break allows this to happen at the junior level, as does the division of breaktimes into activity sessions at the senior level.

In essence, there should be no 'free time' in school, whether in class or out of it.

Classtime

Classrooms should also be properly designed for effective and trouble-free lesson time, and the usefulness of classroom assistants (p. 179) cannot be overemphasised.

Once children leave junior school, it is somehow presumed that they can be seated in a room full of desks and chairs and little else: they are all, without exception, expected to stay on task for the full duration of the lesson. This is clearly asking for trouble if you accept that we are all on a different performance curve. There will always be some children who will not be able to concentrate as well as others, so classrooms should be equipped with alternative activities in order to avoid the possibility of both the gifted and the not so gifted becoming bored.

THE CURRICULUM

The anti-bullying policy should include a statement on how bullying is to be incorporated into the school curriculum.

Subjects

The statement should indicate how bullying is to be approached within a variety of subjects. It should not be accepted that it is going to be addressed only during lessons on personal and social education or in RE, any more than it should be regarded as a permeative element in all subjects. As many subjects as possible should at some time tackle bullying as an issue in its own right within their syllabus.

In addition, the beneficial impact that outdoor pursuits and physical discipline may have in helping both bullies and victims to reassess their perception of themselves (a task in which the counsellor-therapist may be involved (see p. 178)) cannot be overemphasised. Every child should be required to attend at least one week's residential outdoor pursuits course during each school year.

Affective education
The curriculum should also contain a statement regarding the school's recognition not only of its cognitive but also of its affective components. In other words, schools should not only teach facts, figures and techniques: they should also promote an awareness of feeling and an appreciation of the sensitivities and viewpoints of others. Teachers should include in their preparation books three standing orders under the heading 'Aims':

1 to teach knowledge and techniques;
2 to highlight moral and ethical issues;
3 to stimulate an appreciation of the feelings involved in the lessons—either in the subjects being studied or in the pupils who are studying them—and in the process to promote understanding of others and enhanced self-esteem.

THE GROUPING OF CHILDREN

1 By age
Schools should consider the part that their policy of dividing children into groups may play in the promotion of bullying. Since a great deal of bullying occurs when older children come into contact with younger ones, keeping children in their own age groups enables those who are having difficulty to maintain some sense of self-worth. This helps to prevent a deterioration in their behaviour.

2 By ability?
Some schools make the decision not to divide children within a certain age band according to their ability. They see that this is a way of avoiding the possibility of those who are less able feeling inferior. They think that if they were to stream the children according to ability, they would be promoting the difficulties experienced by both bullies and victims.

Mixed-ability grouping has been found to promote the interests of less able children. Working in small groups, more able children can support others, teaching them how to negotiate sensibly and how to reach a consensus of opinion (Chapter 6). Less able children in such situations have gained in confidence to the point where their reading skills, for example, have improved dramatically, and we know that with increased self-confidence the victim's predicament in particular can be alleviated.

THE PART THAT CHILDREN CAN PLAY

Children themselves should be instrumental in the development of the anti-bullying policy. Apart from becoming involved through the curriculum, they should be represented at the policy meetings of the Parent–Teacher Association. A system of class representation, with elections of officers, would not only serve this purpose but could be part of the system adopted for the reporting of bullying episodes. Children are more likely to express their concerns to a peer than to an adult.

In some schools children have been allowed to establish bullying courts, where they and not adults decide upon guilt and administer sanctions. Bullies are deterred not so much by the sanctions as by the ignominy of having to appear before their peers in a formalised setting.

In other schools it has been found appropriate for older and more responsible children to be given workshop training on aspects of bullying, to receive reports of bullying and then decide whom to consult. Another initiative has been for pupils in a secondary school to write to the incoming pupils from junior school asking about their fears and apprehensions. When bullying was mentioned, prospective pupils were reassured on personal safety by being supplied with details of the measures taken against bullies. This exercise also established the status quo in the minds of the writers.

The involvement of children in the development of an anti-bullying policy is well worth considering, but the nature of their involvement needs to be carefully examined. Bullying courts, for example, may be thought to be too formal a way of approaching the matter. Unless the court were closely monitored it could severely alienate the bully, and diminish the notion that adults are in charge of children's behaviour.

STAFFING

Each year a new group of pupils enters a school, and it is hard to envisage the situation arising where an anti-bullying policy will cease to be needed. There will always be some children who are more vulnerable than others, who will either bully or be bullied.

But while it may be relatively simple to devise a policy, it is not so easy to implement it over any length of time. Although there may be no difficulty in getting parents, teachers, children and anyone else involved in the life of the school to agree on the policy, the danger is that unless someone is given the specific responsibility to implement and revise it, it will drift into no-man's land and become yet another statement of intent.

A tripartite management team

Three specialists should be appointed for every five hundred pupils. This team would not only promote, maintain and develop the anti-bullying policy, it would also establish and maintain an acceptable level of affective education.

1   *The countering-bullying coordinator*

The countering-bullying coordinator (CBC) would be a teacher who would have undertaken courses on or related to bullying and who would perform the following paid responsibilities in addition to holding a teaching position:

1   to prepare an anti-bullying policy in consultation with parents, teachers and children;
2   to ensure that the policy is implemented;
3   to revise it annually in consultation with parents, teachers and children.

Episodes of bullying would not be referred to the CBC— he would remain outside any referral system.

2   *The human relations specialist*

Teacher training courses should include the opportunity for all teachers to learn how to deal with difficult children; they should also offer optional specialist training in human relations and family affairs. Teachers would select this option in addition to another subject.

Every school should employ such a specialist. He would teach his other subject for half a week to avoid assuming the stigma attached to full-time 'social workers', and he would have the following responsibilities:

1   to liaise with feeder schools regarding potentially difficult children;
2   to liaise with the homes of these children;
3   to liaise with the counsellor-therapist (below) about individual children who need or already receive special help;
4   to liaise with the receiving teachers;
5   to liaise with the CBC over the implementation of the anti-bullying policy;
6   to provide in-service training in the management of children with emotional problems and associated learning and behavioural difficulties in the classroom, the affective aspects of the curriculum, family matters, bullying, counselling skills and teaching styles.

The in-service training would be mandatory for teachers, their assistants and other ancillaries such as dinner ladies and midday supervisors. The latter, in particular, often suffer from a sense of low status. In-service training can give them a sense of purpose and self-confidence, with the result that thcy can assert their authority more effectively in the playground.

Teaching styles is included as a subject in the in-service programme because many teachers are unaware of the fact that they adopt a bullying style as they are teaching. In every school there is usually at least one member of staff who promotes bullying behaviour among children in this way.

Bullying episodes would not be referred to the human relations specialist who, like the CBC, would remain outside the referral system, observing the anti-bullying policy from the human-relations point of view and contributing to its effectiveness by making his observations known at its annual review.

3   The counsellor-therapist

Teacher training colleges should offer options in counselling and therapy. One such full-time specialist should be appointed for every five hundred pupils, and her duties would be:

1   to provide counselling or therapy for those pupils recommended by the human relations specialist;
2   to facilitate in-service training in counselling skills;
3   to provide a counselling service for parents.

The work of the counsellor-therapist would be highly confidential. Only in cases where disclosures pointed to abuse would information be passed to the head. A child would be informed of these conditions at the beginning of his sessions.

The counsellor-therapist would not be part of any disciplinary process involving bullying episodes. A child referred to her would know that attendance was not a form of punishment. Any disclosures relating to the past would be initiated by the child, with the therapist focusing on the here and now. She would use a variety of therapies, but would centre her work with both bullies and victims on four main elements:

a   Personal assessment

The child would be encouraged to appreciate the significant people, places and events in his life. His positive personal qualities would be examined, and he would be encouraged to see himself as a worthwhile person.

b   Personal discipline

To generate a sense of willpower, disciplined physical exercise would be encouraged. Regular schedules of exercise would be detailed, and his level of achievement would stretch the child to the point where he would begin to sense his self. As already noted, disciplined physical exercise is known to promote physiological change conducive to a sense of calmness and well-being. The victim would feel better because of greater confidence in his physical ability, and the bully would feel more in control of his impulsivity.

c   The ideal model

A child may aspire to an ideal model that is totally unrealistic, which may make him frustrated and unhappy and may promote his aggression or passivity. By looking at his personal heroes the therapist may help him to come to a realistic appraisal of what he might like to be. Part of this process would be to help him to appreciate how others see him.

d   Personal control

When a child has gained sufficient confidence in himself he may be encouraged to think of how he is separate from his emotions—he may be taught how to recognise his emotions and control them.

This final stage would be reached after extensive work on the first three elements of the programme. If it were rushed into, the child might disclaim all responsibility for his emotions rather than assuming control over them. And if victims and bullies can be strengthened to the point where they feel that they have control not only over their emotions but also over their circumstances, the therapist will have achieved her aim.

Classroom assistants

If the class teacher is to avoid behavioural problems, she must organise her classroom so that it is attractive and must be able to present pupils with a variety of appropriate alternative activities. If the classroom environment is pleasant, the behaviour of pupils softens in parallel. If pupils who have completed work to the best of their ability, whether they be bright or less able, have alternatives to turn to, they will not become disruptive.

If those who are experiencing learning difficulties can be given personal assistance before they become frustrated and aggressive, or if they can be deflected into appropriate activities, then the possibility of disruptive, bullying behaviour is minimised.

Classroom assistants can be trained to make all of this possible. Without such assistance the class teacher will find it extremely difficult to meet the needs of bullies and victims. It has proved to be an efficient way of enhancing pupil performance and behaviour, and assistants are particularly cost-effective when compared with other forms of Special Education—which, if they were *not* employed, might be the only alternative for difficult children such as bullies and victims.

THE PROCEDURE FOR DEALING WITH BULLYING

It is important for staff to be clear about the procedure to be followed when they encounter an episode of bullying, and for this to be included in the school's anti-bullying policy. Here are some guiding principles around which a more precise set of instructions can be woven:

1 At the centre of teachers' concern should be the safety and protection of the victim.

2 If they need to intervene physically, they must only hold a child; under no circumstances should they strike him or her.

3 They should send for assistance.

4 The bully should be told to report to a specific place.

5 When the victim is safe with someone else, the bully should be interviewed (Chapter 8).

6 Then the victim should be interviewed (Chapter 8).

7 The parents of both parties should be informed that an incident has occurred and that it has been dealt with. If they wish to see the teacher about what happened, she would be happy to talk to them.

8 If the outcome of the process is unsatisfactory the teacher should refer the matter to the head, who may then decide to interview the bully and possibly speak to his or her parents.

9 The human relations specialist should be informed, and he may refer the child to the counsellor-therapist.

10 The incident should be recorded in an incident book where patterns of behaviour are regularly monitored by the human relations specialist. The information recorded would be based on the questions asked in relation to the investigative interviews (Chapter 8).

CONCLUSION

In schools where an anti-bullying policy has been designed and implemented, bullying has decreased considerably. It is clear that it can be stifled by counter-prevailing forces—that is, by other children and adults. If they can become involved in actively working against bullying, a permanent system of control will be in place.

Teachers and parents can help in this process by designing an infrastructure that will provide children with easy and comfortable lines of communication. Extra benefits may be that future generations will develop greater trust in adults, and that more children will find it easier to live with the bully. For the bully will not cease to exist: there always will be children who are excessively aggressive and dominant, and some who are more vulnerable than others. Moreover it will always be the case, and should be, that adults are not in a position to supervise them continually.

Adults have a second duty: not only are they responsible for designing a system that will protect the victim from the bully, but they must also protect the bully and the victim from themselves. To do this, they must examine their attitude to bullies and victims; they must consider their own needs and the needs of all children. In the light of their findings they should contemplate how they might manage the bully and the victim, and how they might deal with them in a consistent and meaningful way.

I hope that this book has helped you to do this. If it has only raised more questions about bullying in your mind, though, it will have served its purpose. Are there any aspects of human behaviour to which we are not still searching for the answers? But as a mature, well informed and compassionate adult you may well be inspired to act not only in the interests of the child at the centre of your concern but in the interests of future generations.

Appendix A:
Unacceptable Measures

Although it is sometimes necessary to punish children, you should always concentrate on rewarding them when they are behaving well (Chapter 5). When you do need to face them with the consequences of their behaviour you should be aware that children have rights. Although it may seem unnecessary to mention the following unacceptable measures, professionals should look very carefully at their practice: for example, knowing that a child needs spectacles and not arranging an appointment for her or informing her parents could be regarded as withholding medical treatment.

Parents need to know that some of these measures have been specifically listed as unacceptable in order to protect children in boarding schools or children's homes. They should appreciate the need for such measures, and be reassured by them should their child be a boarder. The measures provide a useful subject for debate when partners are deciding on a suitable selection of sanctions for their child. For example, how often do parents stop their child going out as a punishment, and how often do they withhold his pocket money when he is naughty?

1 Corporal punishment
Corporal punishment is defined as the intentional application of force as punishment. You are not allowed to slap, push or punch a child as a response to her violence. You *can* take physical action that may avert the possibility of immediate danger or personal injury to the child, others, yourself or property, but any force used must be moderate and reasonable.

2 Deprivation of food and drink

A child should never be denied access to the range of food and drink normally available to him. Mealtime consequences should therefore always allow for the normal intake of food.

3 Denial of access to parents or relatives

If you are a professional, you should plan the visits that a parent may make to her child, recognising the need that he will always have for regular contact with his natural home. You should never restrict his access to his parents or relatives as a punishment.

4 Use of accommodation to restrict liberty

Professionals should make sure that a child's accommodation is safe and secure from intruders. They are allowed to keep her on the premises when they consider that she will be a danger to herself or others. They should never confine her to accommodation as punishment.

5 Intentional deprivation of sleep

A child should never be denied sleep. If she is awake and unable to sleep she may be removed from a bedroom or dormitory in order that others may sleep, but only until such time as she herself is ready to do so. She should not be stood in a corridor or subjected to physical activities in an attempt to tire her out.

6 Fines

Fines should never be used as punishment for unacceptable behaviour, although a child may be fined in order that property can be repaired or replaced.

7 Intimate physical searches

You may search a child's clothes—but this should never be done as a punishment, only ever as a safety measure. You are never allowed to search his body.

8 The withholding of medication or medical treatment

You should never deny a child access to any medical treatment (including dentistry).

Appendix B:
Sources of Information and Help

Parents whose child is involved in bullying should have the courage to share their concern with a friend or neighbour (Chapter 1). They should never hesitate to speak to their child's teacher; if this proves unfruitful, they should approach the head and then if necessary the school governors. These people are there to help parents when they or their child are experiencing difficulty—it is one of their principal duties. Professionals should never think that they can understand and deal (on their own) with all the problems that children may present. They should consult their colleagues and devise a whole-school behaviour policy (Chapter 10) in which all staff are involved. Educational psychologists and other specialists should be consulted: they are employed primarily for this purpose.

Parents and professionals are the greatest source of practical information and help available to each other, especially when they are conjointly involved in an active anti-bullying policy. In addition, there are national bodies which can provide extremely useful advice and support for parents and professionals attempting to deal with bullying:

Advisory Centre for Education (ACE)
for advice and information: 0171 354 8321
Weekdays 2.00–5.00 p.m.
Useful, inexpensive pamphlets and booklets available.

Childline
For advice and information:
London: 0171 239 1000
Midlands: 01602 691199
Scotland: 0141 551 1123
Wales: 01792 480111
Helpline for children: 0811 1111

Inter-Link
For advice and information: 01504 271 257
Helpline for children: 01504 271257

Kidscape
Helpline for parents and schools: 0171 730 3300
Mondays and Wednesdays 9.30–5.00 p.m.

National Children's Home
For advice and information: 0171 226 2033
Helpline for families and young people:
Leeds: 0113 2456456
London: 0181 514 1177
Maidstone: 01622 756677
Preston: 01772 824006

Organisation for Parents Under Stress (OPUS)
For advice and information: 01268 757077
Helpline for parents: 01268 757077

Wolverhampton Anti-Bullying Project
For advice and information: 01902 757513
Helpline for parents and children: 01902 757513

Survey service
In Chapter 10 I suggested that schools might initiate an anti-bullying campaign by undertaking a survey, and that this could best be done by using a professional service. A contact address for this purpose is:

Survey Service (Bullying)
Department of Psychology, PO Box 603, Western Bank, Sheffield S10 1UR.

Consultancy service
Another way of initiating an anti-bullying campaign might be to hire the services of an expert who could provide an inspirational keynote lecture or workshop. An acknowledged expert on behavioural problems and bullying in particular is:
Mr D. P. Tattum
Countering-Bullying Unit, Cardiff Institute of Higher Education, Cardiff CF2 6DX.

Appendix C:
Useful, Practical Publications

Action Against Bullying: A Support Pack for Schools, Margaret Johnstone, Pamela Munn and Lynne Edwards (1991), Scottish Council for Research in Education, Scottish Office Education Department.   A pack of excellent practical material designed for use by individuals, families and professional groups. Included in the pack is a booklet, *Bullying and How to Fight It: A Guide for Families*, by Andrew Mellor.

Bullies and Victims in Schools, Valerie E. Besag (1989), Open University Press.   Regarded by many as the standard work on bullying: not only does it provide a detailed account of the nature of bullying, it also gives a full description of the many practical ways in which both parents and schools may deal with the problem.

Bullying: An Annotated Bibliography of Literature and Resources, Alison Skinner (1992), National Youth Agency.   Although the title may give the impression that it is not a very practical book, it will be invaluable for both parents and teachers. It provides lists of resources for all kinds of information relating to bullying, plus detailed descriptions of material that may be used either in the school curriculum or at home. Parents and teachers who want to know how to approach bullying either directly or indirectly will begin to find the answers here.

Bullying: Don't suffer in silence. Department of Education (1994), HMSO. This is the pack for all schools that wish to know what the inspector might be looking for. Based on the Sheffield Anti-Bullying Project and the Playgrounds Project (Calouste Gulbenkian Foundation, UK), the pack is essential reading for all professionals.

Bullying: A Practical Guide to Coping for Schools, ed. Michelle Elliot (1991), Longman.   A compendium of research information and practical advice that both parents and professionals will find extremely useful.

Helping Children Cope with Bullying, Sarah Lawson (1994), Sheldon Press.   An excellent book for both parents and teachers who are searching for detailed practical solutions.

Helping the Aggressive Child, Alan Train (1993), Souvenir Press.   There is a fine line to be drawn between the highly aggressive child, the bully and the victim. This book is essential reading if you want to develop an appreciation of why children behave as they do and discover how you might help them. A companion publication to this one, it encourages you to develop your own personal approach to dealing with difficult children.

Bibliography

Assagioli, R. (1975). *Psychosynthesis*. Turnstone Press, London.

Bee, H. (1969). *The Developing Child*. Harper & Row, New York.

Besag, V. (1989). *Bullies and Victims in School*. Open University Press, Milton Keynes.

Bettelheim, B. (1987). *The Good Enough Parent*. Thames & Hudson, London.

Blatchford, P. (1989). *Playtime in the Primary School: Problems and Improvements*. National Foundation for Educational Research in England and Wales (NFER), Nelson, Walton-on-Thames, Surrey.

Blatchford, P. and Sharp, S. (eds.) (1994). *Breaktime in the School: Understanding and Changing Playground Behaviour*. Routledge, London.

Blos, P. (1979). *The Adolescent Passage: Developmental Issues*. New York University Press.

Byrne, B. (1994). *Coping with Bullying in School*. Cassell, London.

Chazan, M. (1988). Bullying in the Infant School, in D. Tattum and D. Lane (eds.), *Bullying in Schools*. Trentham Books, Stoke-on-Trent.

Elliot, M. (1991). *Bullying: A Practical Guide to Coping for Schools*. Longman, Harlow, Essex.

Emery, R. E. (1982). Interparental Conflict and the Children of Discord and Divorce. *Psychological Bulletin* 92 (310–30).

Erikson, E. H. (1968). *Identity, Youth and Crisis*. W. W. Norton, New York.

Evans, J. (1989). *Children at Play: Life in the School Playground*. Deakin University Press, Australia.

Fromm, E. (1987). *The Anatomy of Human Destructiveness*. Pelican Books, London.

Garman, T., Hutchinson, D. and Trimble, J. (1994). *Reading in Reform: The Avon Collaborative Reading Project*. (NFER), Nelson, Walton-on-Thames, Surrey.

Gelles, R. J. (1987). *The Violent Home*, 2nd edn. Sage, London.

Golding, J. and Rush, D. (1986). Temper Tantrums and Other Behavioural Problems, in N. R. Butler and J. Golding (eds.), *From Birth to Five*. Pergamon Press, Oxford.

Greiger, R. (1982). Anger Problems, in R. Greiger and I. Z. Greiger (eds.), *Emotional Disturbance*. Human Sciences Press, New York.

Hall, E. and Hall, C. (1988). *Human Relations in Education*. Routledge, London.

Heinemann, P. P. (1973). *Mobbing: gruppevold blant barn og voksne* (Bullying: Group Violence among Children and Adults). Gyldendal, Oslo.

Hoghughi, M. (1988). *Treating Problem Children*. Sage, London.

Huesmann, R., Evan, L., Lefkowitz, M. and Walder, L. (1984). Stability of Aggression over Time and Generation. *Developmental Psychology* 20 (1120–34).

Johnstone, M., Munn, P. and Edwards, L. (1991). *Action against Bullying: A Support Pack for Schools*. Scottish Council for Research in Education, Edinburgh.

Keise, C. (1992). *Sugar and Spice? Bullying in Single-sex Schools*. Trentham Books, Stoke-on-Trent.

La Fontaine, J. (1991). *Bullying: A Child's View*. Calouste Gulbenkian Foundation, London.

Laslett, R. (1982). A Children's Court for Bullies. *Special Education* 9, 1 (9–11).

Lawson, S. (1994). *Helping Children Cope with Bullying*. Sheldon Press, London.

Lorenz, K. (1966). *On Aggression*. Methuen, London.

Manning, M. and Sluckin, P. (1984). The Function of Aggression in the Pre-school and Primary Years, in N. Frude and H. Gault (eds), *Disruptive Behaviour in Schools*. J. Wiley, New York.

Marcia, J. E. (1980). Identity in Adolescence, in J. Edelson (ed.), *Handbook of Adolescent Psychiatry*. J. Wiley, New York.

190   *The Bullying Problem*

Mellor, A. (1990). *Bullying in Scottish Secondary Schools*, Spotlight no. 23. Scottish Council for Research in Education.

Mitchell, A. R. K. (1978). *Violence in the Family*. Wayland, Hove, Sussex.

Olweus, D. (1978). *Aggression in the Schools: Bullies and Whipping Boys*. Hemisphere Press, Washington DC.

Olweus, D. (1981). Bullying among Schoolboys, in N. Cantwell (ed.), *Children and Violence*. Akademilitteratur, Stockholm.

Olweus, D. (1993). *Bullying at School: What We Know and What We Can Do*. Blackwell, Oxford.

O'Moore, A. M. and Hillery, B. (1989). Bullying in Dublin Schools. *The Irish Journal of Psychology* 10, 3 (426–41).

Patterson, G. R. Lithman, R. A. and Bricker, W. (1987). *Assertive Behaviour in Children: A Step towards a Theory of Aggression*. Monographs of the Society for Research in Child Development 32(5) (1–43).

Redl, F. and Wineman, D. (1965). *Controls from Within*. Free Press, New York.

Ross, C. and Ryan, A. (1990). *Can I Stay in Today Miss? Improving the School Playground*. Trentham Books, Stoke-on-Trent.

Rutter, M. (1987). Psychology of Resilience and Protective Mechanisms. *American Journal of Orthopsychiatry* 57 (317–31).

Sharp, S. and Smith, P. (1991). Bullying in UK Schools: The DFE Sheffield Bullying Project. *Early Child Development and Care* 77 (47–55).

Sluckin, A. (1981). *Growing up in the Playground: The Social Development of Children*. Routledge & Kegan Paul, London.

Smith, P. (1991). The Silent Nightmare: Bullying and Victimisation in School Peer Groups. *The Psychologist* 4 (243–8).

Smith, P. K. and Thompson, D. (eds.) (1991). *Practical Approaches to Bullying*. David Fulton, London.

Storr, A. (1968). *Human Aggression*. Penguin Books, Harmondsworth, Middlesex.

Tattum, D. P. and Herbert, G. (1993). *Countering Bullying:*

Initiatives in Schools and Local Authorities. Trentham Books, Stoke-on-Trent.

Tattum, D. P. and Lane, D. A. (1989). *Bullying in Schools.* Trentham Books, Stoke-on-Trent.

Train, A. G. (1993). *Helping the Aggressive Child.* Souvenir Press, London.

Train, D. W. (1992). The Ideal Olympics. Unpublished paper. Gladbury, Worcestershire.

Wedge, P. and Essen, J. (1973). *Born to Fail.* Arrow Books, London.

Whitness, I. and Smith, P. K. (1993). *A Survey of the Nature and Extent of Bullying in Junior/Middle and Secondary Schools.* Educational Research, London.

Winnicott, D. W. (1958). *Aggression in Relation to Emotional Development,* in *Collected Papers.* Tavistock, London.

Index